Manga High

Literacy, Identity, and Coming of Age in an Urban High School

Michael Bitz

HARVARD EDUCATION PRESS
CAMBRIDGE, MASSACHUSETTS

Library of Congress Control Number: 2008942552
Paperback ISBN: 978-1-934742-18-1
Library Edition ISBN: 978-1-934742-19-8

Published by Harvard Education Press,
an imprint of the Harvard Education Publishing Group
Harvard Education Press
8 Story Street
Cambridge, MA 02138

Cover Design: Perry Lubin

The typefaces used in this book are ITC Eras and Janson Text.

Dedicated to all the students and staff—

past and present—who have

participated in the comic book club

at Martin Luther King Jr. High School

AND

To my family, especially my parents

AND

Most of all, to Allison

Contents

List of Figures

Foreword

Françoise Mouly

COMICS TEND TO ELICIT strong love or hate reactions. In their heyday in the 1950s, comics were the first truly mass-media phenomenon to cater to Baby Boomer children. The lead titles sold more than 6 million copies a week, and, thanks to pass-along readership, were read by many more millions of nine- to twelve-year-olds (the prime comic book reading age). The new medium of comic books burst into the second half of the twentieth century with very little oversight, fostering at the same time phenomenal creativity and some extremely lurid horror and crime comics. By 1954, comics were denounced in congressional hearings as one of the main causes of juvenile delinquency. As the outcry grew—that comics were crude and could only pervert the mind of their readers—educators ripped them out of the hands of students. We have since heard similar denunciations about rock and roll, rap music, and video games, but these outcries never quite reached the frenzy that led to comic book burnings and more than a hundred laws proposed to ban comics. After the mid-1960s, comics for children pretty much atrophied into safe and sanitized shadows of their former selves.

Flash forward fifty years to the present. Comics have long ceased to be a large-scale mass medium, but they are now accepted as a valid form for art, literature, and personal expression. Back in 1980, when I published the first chapter of *Maus*, Art Spiegelman's story of his parents' ordeal during World War II, the idea of a comic book about the Holocaust was outrageous; to most people it was actually sacrilegious. Now, more than twenty years after the publication of *Maus* in book form, comics routinely receive literary prizes, are displayed in museums and bookstores, and the "Graphic Novel" section has become the cornerstone of many libraries. In the book publishing industry, graphic novels (GNs) are beloved: they are one of the few areas of publishing that has been expanding rather than declining.

Yet, even in this context, Michael Bitz, an educator who proposes to use comics as a teaching tool, stands out. Comics have always benefited from the advocacy of their highly literate and passionate fans, but Bitz is not just trying to defend comics, he wants to bulldoze over what remains of the deeply entrenched prejudices against them. As founder of the Comic Book Project, he wants teachers not just to allow or tolerate comics—or the Japanese variant, *manga*—in the schools but to embrace them, advocate for them, and even help their students discover the medium, since not all children nowadays even know what comics are. And he wants all the kids, the artistically inclined and the reluctant readers, together with the nerds and the jocks, to spend hours after school making their own. As revolutionary as it is, his premise is simple: kids intuitively love comics, so they can and should be used in the educational environment.

I recognize the paradoxes inherent in what Bitz proposes, since I'm now advocating that comics can be for children as ardently as I once insisted that they were not just for kids. I recently launched TOON Books, a collection of comics for young readers, built on the fact that comics have a unique ability to draw emerging readers into a story through the drawings. Visual narratives help kids crack the code that allows literacy to flourish, and many of the issues that stump struggling readers are instantly clarified by comics' inviting format. Barbara Tversky, professor of psychology at Stanford University, and an adviser to TOON Books, explains:

> Comics use a broad range of sophisticated devices for communication. They are similar to face-to-face interactions, in which meaning is derived not solely from words, but also from gestures, intonation, facial expressions and props. Comics are more than just illustrated books, but rather make use of a multi-modal language that blends words, pictures, facial expressions, panel-to-panel progression, color, sound effects and more to engage readers in a compelling narrative.[1]

"For kids who may be struggling and for kids who may be new to the English language," says Bitz, "that visual sequence is a very powerful tool."

When he started the Comic Book Project, Michael Bitz acted on a brilliant insight. He realized that among the media to which kids are attracted, comics and manga share a unique characteristic: comics' visibly handmade quality prompts readers to intuitively perceive them as expressions of the voice of their author. Readers are inspired to become authors. This seldom happens to the child who plays video games or watches an animated cartoon, but even kids who don't usually draw are eager to try their hand at manga or comics. And thanks to Bitz's emphasis on having the kids tell stories about their own lives, the authors are doubly motivated. "Because it's their story," he adds, "they want to make it right."

But even if reading comics is fun, making comics is no funny business, as Bitz of course knows. Because children like comics, people tend to think that they are easy to make, but as any cartoonist will tell you, making comics is hard work, more akin to writing poetry than to doodling. Comics do not tolerate vague or fuzzy thinking. They are all about communication.

Regardless of his or her skill level, the student setting out to tell a story in comics has to use metaphorical thinking when building the inferences that will be made by the reader. Take, for example, the deceptively simple drawing by fourth-grader Harry from the Beginning with Children Charter School/The After-School Corporation program in Brooklyn: "Now Francis changes into a good person."

If, instead of creating a comic, Harry had been asked to write about how his character becomes a good person, he may have simply written, "He became nice." But in a comic narrative, pictures must be precise. For his comic, Harry decided to juxtapose the before and after moments in a transformation. He had to think about how to represent a "bad" person versus a "good" one. The most meaningful change between the two drawings is the scowl that turns into a smile, forcing the fourth-grader to reflect on the importance of the face one presents to the world.

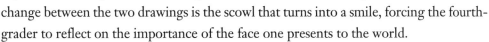

As Bitz relates in *Manga High*, many of the students involved in the Martin Luther King Jr. High School comic book club readily learned to work as a team, each finding a role as writer, artist, inker, or editor. When planning a comic, even the young and unskilled must think rigorously about the story and structure the narrative into its beginning, middle, and end. The fact that drawing is so labor-intensive provides a helpful barrier: because every scene must be drawn, the story must be boiled down to its essence, and each panel in turn should only include the elements that will fit the narrative. If the story describes an interaction on a street corner, the artist will probably only draw the buildings or cars or storefronts that need to be there to indicate where the action takes place. Making a comic or a manga, with their strict conventions, provides an often self-taught course in how to tell a story by distilling it to its essentials.

If you want to tell a story in a comic book form, you are forced to visualize the character, what he looks like, what he is wearing, where he is standing, what time of day it is, whether he is alone or interacting with others. The author/artist will have to define how each character is different from the others, and find a way to distinguish the main characters from the background ones. He or she will have to learn to draw a character in various situations, from different angles, with variable facial expressions. The manga creator will need to be well versed in the intricate conventions of the form. He or she will copy, trace, swipe, and, in looking up references, become part expert, part historian. The budding cartoonist will learn to recognize the difference between what, in his 1845 "Essay on Physiognomy," Rodolphe Töpffer, the inventor of comics, called fixed signs (how skinny or fat a character is, for example) and mutable signs (the facial expression, such as a smile). They will discover what the art historian Ernest Gombrich dubbed "Töpffer's Law," which states that humans' brains impart meaning to every aspect of a visual representation, especially to faces:

> The most astonishing fact about these clues of expression is surely that they may transform almost any shape into the semblance of a living being. Discover expression in the staring eye or gaping jaw of a lifeless form, and what might be called "Töpffer's Law" will come into operation—it will not be classed just as a face but will acquire a definite character and expression, will be endowed with life, with a presence.[2]

Not only will the authors/artists have to choose their character's body shape or height, but they will have to choose his or her hairdo, since all of the details impart meaning. They will have to think of the right dialogue to best express the interactions between characters and move the story along. They will make decisions about balloon placement and lettering size (large letters when characters shout, small ones when they whisper). If they choose to draw a page about a character who has forgotten his lunch money, they're likely to go to the cafeteria to observe how the counter is arranged, where people are standing, and exactly what a cash register looks like. They'll realize how important it is to note which students are in clusters, and which are alone.

In *Manga High*, Bitz describes a project that is the sort of Holy Grail that many an educator pursues. Like the manga club at MLKHS, the afterschool clubs founded through the Comic Book Project have transformed thousands of kids into active learners, communicators, and creators of stories about their own lives. Who would have thought, when they were throwing them on bonfires, that comic books in the hands of a fearless educator could accomplish so much?

—Françoise Mouly
    Editorial Director, TOON Books
    Art Editor, *The New Yorker*

Introduction

The Story Behind the Stories

"WHAT'S OLD IS NEW AGAIN." Whoever coined this phrase very well could have been referring to comic books. The medium that blossomed in the 1930s with iconic superheroes like Superman and Batman is one of the fastest-growing sectors in retail publishing. Comics and graphic novels line bookstore shelves and they are the basis of films ranging from loud blockbusters like *Iron Man* to introspective independents like *Persepolis*. The genre, which the U.S. Congress investigated in the 1950s for instigating juvenile delinquency, is now an accepted and acclaimed literary form garnering Pulitzer Prizes (Art Spiegelman's *Maus*) and nods from the National Book Awards (Gene Luen Yang's *American Born Chinese*).[1]

Amid the newfound commercial enthusiasm over comics is a rapidly growing movement of educators who are embracing the medium as a tool for reading improvement. Many educational publishers have a how-to book on using comics in the classroom.[2] The Maryland State Department of Education has partnered with Disney and the comics distributor Diamond to develop its own comics-based curriculum. Now the American Library Association endorses comics as a valuable tool for reluctant readers. There is even a National Association of Comics Art Educators.[3]

But just as comics themselves have a long history, so does the concept of comics in the classroom. In 1944, the *Journal of Educational Sociology* devoted an entire issue to the educational use of comics, with articles such as "The Comics and Instructional Method."[4] These endeavors were not merely relegated to scholarly journals. In the 1940s, the publishers of Superman connected with educational researcher Robert Thorndike, best known for his Cognitive Ability Test, to create a language-arts workbook in which the Man of Steel battles dangling participles and spelling errors. Perhaps the most lasting example of educational comics was *Classic Comics*—Dickens and Melville (and many others) in comic book form. This series, which was renamed *Classics Illustrated* to disassociate it from the comics medium, could be found in dime stores, drugstores, and later in comics shops, but issues were also distributed with the *Saturday Evening Post* and *Atlantic Monthly*. It was no small press—most of the editions began with a first printing of 250,000 copies, and at its height the series generated monthly sales between $2 million and $5 million dollars. The most popular title, *Ivanhoe*, was reissued twenty-four times over three decades.[5]

What's old is new again, indeed. Several publishers have recently issued classic novels in comic book form.[6] One large test-prep publisher produced a graphic novel featuring three hundred of the most common SAT vocabulary words: "The Psychic Commandos *defiantly* burst through the cargo door . . ."[7] And now, along with grammar lessons, Superman is helping third-graders combat addition and subtraction problems in a workbook, which includes a progress chart with colorful stickers emblazoned with the superhero's yellow and red "S."[8] Not to be left behind, academics are ever more frequently looking to comics and graphic novels as viable educational tools.[9]

About the Comic Book Project

From my perspective as an educator and youth advocate, the comics-in-education movement has been mostly missing the mark since the 1940s through today. While comics can be a motivational bridge to reading, and the comic book is certainly a viable literary form, a more comprehensive—and arguably more authentic—educational approach is to engage children in writing and designing their own comic books and then publishing those works in their schools and communities. This has been the goal of the Comic Book Project (CBP), which I founded in 2001 at a middle school in New York City. Since that time, CBP has grown to encompass over fifty thousand youths across the United States, mostly in high-poverty urban schools and neighborhoods. With the support of Teachers College, Columbia University and Dark Horse Comics,

CBP became a way for underserved children to find a voice in the learning process by creating original writing and artwork about important issues in their lives.

The concept of CBP was born from my work as a graduate assistant working on *Learning In and Through the Arts*, a large-scale research study investigating the academic and social impacts of children's involvement in the arts.[10] That study and others since then demonstrated to me three important factors for successful integration of the arts into the core academic learning environment. First, the arts content must be clearly and explicitly integrated with the academic content.[11] Second, the educational context must be socially relevant; as John Dewey argued over a century ago: "The only true education comes through the stimulation of the child's powers by the demands of the social situations in which he finds himself."[12] Finally, there must be consistent and enthusiastic support from teachers, administrators, parents, students, and community partners for successful arts integration.[13]

CBP launched as a way of initiating wide-scale and sustainable change that meets the three criteria outlined above. More than just a fun and motivational project for children, CBP began as a model for how creative thinking can bolster academic success. A second goal was to support the many inner-city children who rarely have the opportunity to be creative in school due to a lack of resources and an increased focus on standardized test preparation. The CBP concept was simple: children would plan, write, design, and produce original comic books on a socially relevant theme, then publish and distribute their work for other children to use as learning and motivational tools. The project first began in the New York City afterschool community through partnerships with nonprofit organizations like The After-School Corporation, the Children's Aid Society, and the Partnership for After School Education. Through the support of the Cleveland Foundation in 2003, CBP migrated to Cleveland as a school-day initiative where art teachers partnered with English teachers to plan, create, and publish the comics. Then to Philadelphia, Baltimore, Chicago, and on and on . . .

The comic books that children create through CBP have always been a means to the ends of creative thinking, personal expression, literacy development, and community building. Because creativity trumps art skills or writing abilities in this setting, almost every child has found a role in the process. The students often form teams, each with a writer, artist, editor, and inker. The writers draft manuscripts; the artists put forth character designs and panel layouts; the editors proof the grammar, spelling, and writing mechanics; the inkers outline the important words and images. The result has been a convergence of conventional literacy and "new" literacies, social and personal development, parent and community involvement, and individual and cultural tolerance.

CBP's constantly evolving process has elucidated several things about the project specifically and learning in general. First, if students begin with creative thinking, rather than essay writing or figure drawing, then *all* of them can participate—boys, girls, reluctant readers, reluctant drawers, English-language learners, English-language abusers, and even the one with his feet on the desk and a permanently embedded iPod earbud. Second, children can learn extraordinary things from each other by sharing and evaluating the work of peers. For example, in the development of a new superhero, I overheard one fourth-grader say to his friend, "But *why* does Ghetto Boy fly? You gotta get to the *why* of it all." Finally, creating a comic book can be a pathway to conventional and unconventional literacy alike. In the process, children plan the characters; delineate a plot; compose a manuscript; deliberate elements of tone and atmosphere; revise and edit their writing; concentrate on character and story development; correct spelling, grammar, and punctuation; review peer work; share and discuss storylines; and present and publish finalized works. In essence, these students, who in many cases are labeled as "underachieving," thoroughly meet all of the benchmark standards related to literacy and English-language arts.

But in the end, it is the *content* of the student comic books that has made the most lasting impression. The students create comic books about life in the city; their finished products are distinct from the tradition of superheroes saving the world. Many stories focus on the often harsh realities of growing up in the city. The children produce comic books about themselves, their friends, and their concerns about everything from snitching to teen pregnancy. And while many professionally designed comic books feature a hero with a flowing cape and super powers, the children's comic books are often devoid of superheroes. When I asked one fourth-grade student in the East New York neighborhood of Brooklyn why a superhero never appeared in his comic, the boy responded, "Superman don't come here."

About This Book

There are many, many stories to tell from the past years with CBP. Students and teachers in Cleveland who stood up to rising violence in their schools by creating comic books about conflict resolution. A group of special education students at a charter school in Philadelphia who developed and presented comic books about tolerance. Fifth-graders at a Brooklyn afterschool program who used digital photographs of the neighborhood and school as the groundwork for a classroom graphic novel. Incarcerated youths outside of Detroit who wrote and drew about their reflections of the past and hopes for the future. And the Owl and Panther—a group of refugee children in Tucson, who scanned photographs from their home countries, then altered the color prints with sandpaper, small screwdrivers, glue sticks, and markers. The characters in their collective comic book are refugees who are guided throughout the story by a patient owl and a resolute panther through the most difficult situations imaginable: camps, prisons, deserts. The comic book ends with powerful words: "The spirit of the owl and panther inspired these children to be brave and creative. By telling their stories . . . the refugees write themselves out of their darkness."

Nevertheless, in this book I elect to concentrate on the comic book club at Martin Luther King Jr. High School (MLKHS) in New York City. There are several reasons for this decision. First, because I live in New York City, I have had the chance to visit and observe the club frequently. Educators have sent me equally fascinating work from students in Hawaii, Baltimore, San Francisco, and all the other places that CBP has flourished, but I know these students only through the words and ink in their comic books, not personally. Second, this particular comic book club has been thriving for several years. I have seen it grow, and I have witnessed some remarkable, and equally disturbing, events and occurrences in the lives of the children and that of the club itself. Lastly, although I did have a hand in launching and sustaining this club, I have been an outside observer since its inception. The direction of the club is driven by the students, their teacher, and the program staff at the school. I have been welcomed by them all, but as an observer rather than a participant.

In many ways the comic book club at MLKHS is an outlier from the hundreds of other CBP clubs around the United States. The students here are high schoolers; most of the other participants in CBP are elementary and middle schoolers. This high school club does not follow the CBP curriculum or lesson plans, where each session is carefully outlined with a goal, handout, and activity. Rather their process is organic and varies from not only year to year but also student to student. Their teacher—Phil DeJean—is a comics fanatic, whereas most of the educators involved in CBP never imagined themselves helping students to create comic books. Unlike the younger participants who use blank paper and colored pencils to create their comics, many of the MLKHS high schoolers scan their drawings into Adobe Photoshop and colorize them digitally.

But the most dramatic difference, and the subject matter of this book, is the club members' embracing of and devotion to *manga*—Japanese comic books. Aside from the plethora of "How to Draw" guides (and the surprisingly numerous versions of the Bible in manga form), there are only a few thorough sources on the subject of manga: Paul Gravett, Adam Kern, Brigitte Koyama-Richard, and Frederick Schodt.[14] Brent Wilson has demonstrated the close relationship between manga and Japanese youth identity—when young Japanese children are asked to create sequential stories, they draw manga.[15] Masami Toku has explored the historical contexts of manga by focusing on one of many subgenres called *shojo* manga, written specifically for, and often by, young women.[16] Perhaps the best introduction to the medium, however, is manga itself. Classic manga like the spiritual *Clover* by an all-woman manga studio and the intensely complex *Ghost in the Shell* represent just a trickle of the manga ocean that has swept across the world.[17]

Rather than taking an expansive view, this book focuses on the role of manga in the lives of a group of students at one high school in New York City. I divide the book into two parts. The first is an analysis and synthesis of the processes and products of the comic book club; the methodology of the resulting ethnographic study is outlined in appendix B. The second part features profiles of selected students and examples of their work. My hope is that readers will come away from this book with new ideas about literacy, cultural identity, and social development that could have practical applications both in and out of the classroom. I believe that the comic book club at Martin Luther King Jr. High School is a prime example of socially relevant education where creative learning and academic reinforcement are not mutually exclusive. But if nothing else, this book brings to light the work of dedicated high schoolers who—against many odds and without the prodding of adults—read books, write stories, and make art because their lives would be incomplete otherwise. For those of us who struggle daily to engage children in English language arts, here are students who read and write on their own simply because they find such pursuits personally meaningful and rewarding. I believe that this is a lesson for educators worth learning.

Part I

The Story

Chapter One

"Manga Is My Life"

Foundations of the Comic Book Club

THERE ARE TWO HIGH SCHOOLS on Amsterdam Avenue and 66th Street in Manhattan. LaGuardia High School of Music & Art and Performing Arts, on the southwest corner, is rather famous; it was the subject of the 1980s movie and television series *Fame*. One of New York City's nine highly selective "specialized" high schools, LaGuardia is an academic and artistic conservatory for future professional artists, musicians, actors, and dancers, many of whom aim to perform at prestigious Lincoln Center, directly across the avenue. Demographically, LaGuardia is representative of the Upper West Side, the very affluent neighborhood in which it sits. Data from the New York State Department of Education show that in 2005–06, only 1 percent of students at LaGuardia had limited English proficiency, and 17 percent were eligible for free or reduced-priced lunch.[1] As one might imagine, LaGuardia High School is academically strong. The school received an "A" on its 2006–07 progress report from the New York City Department of Education, with a score of 27.7 out of 30 in student performance.[2]

On the other hand, Martin Luther King Jr. High School, on the northwest corner, is somewhat infamous. Several violent incidents have plagued this institution, including a 2002 shooting inside school walls that left two tenth graders in serious condition. In response to persistently poor academic performance, the New York City Department of Education officially closed Martin Luther King Jr. High School in 2005. It is now the Martin Luther King Jr. Educational Campus. Six high schools occupy the giant boxlike structure, each with its own teachers, administrators, and students:

- High School for Law, Advocacy and Community Justice
- High School of Arts and Technology
- Manhattan/Hunter Science High School
- Urban Assembly School for Media Studies
- High School for Arts, Imagination, and Inquiry
- Manhattan Theatre Lab High School

Aggregating the available data for these six schools, Martin Luther King Jr. Educational Campus is a stark contrast to its neighbor, LaGuardia. According to the New York City Department of Education, the student performance in 2006–07 was an average score of 13.2 out of 30. And unlike LaGuardia, which is predominantly white and Asian, this conglomerate of schools is not at all representative of the Upper West Side. In 2005–06, 63 percent of students were eligible for free or reduced-price lunch. In that school year, 90 percent of students were African American or Latino.

Considering these facts, one might imagine that this book, concerning as it does creativity, art, writing, social development, and community-building, is about LaGuardia High School. After all, creativity is at the core of what transpires at LaGuardia, and it is known to graduate some of New York City's most artistic and imaginative students. But, in fact, this book is about Martin Luther King Jr. High School. I'll be referring to this school as MLKHS, using its now-defunct name for two reasons (neither of which concern the big block letters still on the face of the building: "Martin Luther King Jr. High School"). First, for the initial two years of this project (2004 and 2005), the school *was* Martin Luther King Jr. High School. If you were to ask students in the third and fourth years of the project (2006 and 2007) which of the six high schools they attend, most would simply say, "MLK." Second, this book is about an afterschool program that brought students from all six schools together. During the school day, they were separated by floor. Students wandering from one floor to another (that is, one school to another) would be in big trouble. After school, however, the students were a unified group, working together to learn not just about language and literacy but also about themselves, where they came from, and where they were going.

Opening Doors and Building Bridges

The afterschool program at MLKHS is called Opening Doors and Building Bridges, an initiative launched in 1999 by the Lincoln Square Business Improvement District. Additional funding for Opening Doors has been provided by the federal 21st Century Community Learning Centers initiative and The After-School Corporation (TASC), a nonprofit organization dedicated to sustaining afterschool programming in New York City. Opening Doors provides students at MLKHS with academic support including tutoring, homework assistance, college application review, and SAT preparation. The program also offers supervised activities, including chess, yoga, and hip-hop dance. Like most afterschool programs in New York City, Opening Doors is a safe haven. It is a place where students can receive help with not only schoolwork but also life issues—peer relationships, problems at home, the many other struggles of being a teenager in a difficult city. Especially now, with competition for resources and space between the six schools in the building, Opening Doors provides a sense of stability and unity among the students who attend the program. As one student told me, "We all walk through the same metal detector to get into this place; we might as well help each other on the way out."

In 2004, I was attempting to open doors and build bridges of my own for the Comic Book Project (CBP). In the 2004–05 school year, CBP was implemented in afterschool programs at elementary and middle schools across New York City through funding from TASC and, of all things, the United States Environmental Protection Agency. Not coincidentally, the theme of the student comic books that year was environmental awareness and protection. Why the environment as a theme for youth in New York City? Young urban dwellers often assume that the environment, being related to nature, is far removed from the inner city. They learn about polar bears struggling in Alaska and depleted krill populations at the South Pole. But regarding humans, it is urban dwellers who are most immediately affected by pollution and disregard for the environment. The goal of this CBP implementation was to encourage children to think critically about the environment by incorporating the issues into written and artistic narratives—comic books—that would be experienced by thousands of other children and adults in their communities. The project would culminate in a printed compendium of selected student work; exhibits of the comic books for students, parents, educators, and community members; and online galleries representing every participating student.

Soon after the 2004 school year began, I received an e-mail from Rebecca Fabiano, the director of Opening Doors and Building Bridges. Rebecca always had her eye out for interesting programs, and she wanted to explore the possibilities of launching a comic book club at MLKHS. We met, and she explained her intention to replicate the process and outcomes of CBP for the students at MLKHS—to engage her high schoolers in planning and creating original comic books, then publishing and distributing those works in the school and beyond.

Personally, I was a bit skeptical at the outset, knowing that the lesson plans and materials of CBP had been designed for younger learners. But she convinced me: "Give some of these kids blank paper and a pencil, and they will create the most amazing things you have ever seen." After flipping through some doodles and sketches confiscated from an SAT preparation class, I was won over. Not only was the art dynamic, but the writing represented sophistication beyond the grade levels at which these students were supposed to be struggling. Clearly an educational opportunity was being missed. These high schoolers were motivated to write. Of course, it was a bit ironic that their writing transpired during a review class for the new essay portion of the SAT.

Welcome to Manga

I did notice some unique things about the sketches. The drawings seemed to be intended for a comic book . . . but then again they looked entirely foreign to me. The characters had enormous eyes, with pupils nearly as large. Their hair was spiked and highly styled, as though the cartoon figures had spent just as much time primping as the artists must have expended in drawing those intricate details. Instead of the capes and shields donned by most of the environmental superheroes created by younger students in CBP, these characters wore chic clothes. It was difficult to distinguish some of the male characters from the females, but they all appeared in trendy embroidered jeans and fitted shirts or custom suits with upturned collars, like the characters in figure 1.1, created by a female MLKHS student.

I didn't know it yet, but I had just experienced my first *manga*, the Japanese style and form of the comic book medium. Later I would learn the extraordinary history of manga, with its roots in narrative picture scrolls dating as far back as the twelfth century in ancient Kyoto.[3] Modern manga blossomed just after World War II, influenced by the superhero comic books brought to Japan by American soldiers on duty there.

FIGURE 1.1 MANGA CREATED BY A MLKHS STUDENT

Like popular comics by Marvel and DC Comics, manga is character-driven. It is an illustrated and written sequential narrative built on rectangular boxes, or panels, that frame a story from beginning to end. There are many parallels to American comic books, but there are also some fundamental differences, as I gathered from the serious inquisition I got from Angel, the tenth-grade African American girl whose sketchbook I was examining.

"Do you know Miwa Ueda?" Angel asked.

I stammered, "Um, no, I don't know him personally."

"He's a *she*. You know, *Peach Girl*?"

Angel might as well have been speaking Japanese to me. In fact, I soon learned that she did know some Japanese words, which she had gleaned from the collection of manga that spilled from her backpack. Among the dozen or so books were Naoko Takeuchi's *Sailor Moon* and Kosuke Fujishima's *Oh My Goddess!*[4] I plucked one of the volumes from the floor, opened the cover, and thumbed to the first page, which had a large stop sign and the words: "Stop! This book reads from right to left"—manga translated from its original Japanese begins on the right. I flipped the book over and began to read the whimsical story of a fully licensed goddess named Belldandy, who dons a special earring that limits her goddess powers on Earth. Female characters like Belldandy often play the central role in manga; moreover, manga is often created by women artists, known in Japan as *mangaka*. All this I learned within a few minutes from Angel. I was beginning to realize that the high schooler before me was not just a manga fan—she was a scholar. "So you're really into this," I said to her.

"Manga is my life," she gushed.

Manga and Identity

Perhaps it is surprising that an African American girl in New York City identifies with the Japanese art form and literature of manga, rather than hip-hop music, MySpace, or any other medium typically associated with urban teens. After all, Angel had never been to Japan. She did not have any Japanese schoolmates. In fact, she had only met one or two Japanese people in her life. And while manga has become a worldwide phenomenon, it is distinctly representative of national Japanese identity. Brent Wilson discovered an inextricable link between manga and Japanese children, who at the age of six created manga when asked to design a sequential story.[5] Masami Toku reported the dynamic influence of manga on Japanese adolescents, who buck the trend of waning interest in artistic activities as children get older.[6] The Japan Ministry of Education has even included manga in its national curriculum.[7]

But why in New York? These high schoolers were passionate about the manga stories and the characters contained therein. This was not a convenient escape from reality—it was authentic engagement in language and literature. From an educator's perspective, this is extraordinary. As we struggle to engage children in reading, the youths at MLKHS were engrossed in books. They were reading on their own time and of their own volition, and they were doing so at an insatiable pace. These students anxiously awaited forthcoming issues from manga publishers like Tokyopop and Viz. It was uncanny how much the students loved to read, especially considering the poor grades that most of them received in their English language arts classes.

My four years of work at MLKHS shed light on the connections between urban teenagers such as Angel and the manga generated thousands of miles away, both geographically and figuratively. One point of consideration is rooted in personal, cultural, and societal expectations. These teenagers were butting against what they were "supposed" to be, and all the terms that a stranger on the subway might have applied to them at first sight: thug, gangbanger, gangsta . . . the list of derogatory epithets could fill pages. By embracing manga, the teens entered what Mary Louise Pratt has defined as a "contact zone," where a person meets, clashes, and grapples with accepted societal norms and practices.[8] These high school students defined—or redefined—themselves by how they chose to spend their time, with whom they spent that time, and the arts and media that they consumed in those hours. As Angel demonstrated, her devotion to manga was more than a fashionable fad. At the time, she was consumed with manga because it said something important to her and her sense of identity.

Second, the club at MLKHS was founded in the culture surrounding manga. In Japan, reading manga is one part of the experience. But Japanese children and adults also spend extensive time creating their own manga individually or in clubs called *dojinshi* groups or circles. They self-publish their original comic books online, create low-budget printed versions, or distribute the originals to friends and other fans. The students at MLKHS consciously mimicked the Japanese practice in their own manga production club. In one sense, the MLKHS club related to the students' desires to embrace manga in its totality, including the Japanese practice of self-production and publishing. But for most of the students, the club was an opportunity to be creative.

The students did not have regular art classes, and creative writing was a minor component of the high school English language arts curriculum, especially as the school year approached the time for the state-mandated Regents exams required for graduation.

Again, from an educator's perspective, the opportunity for children to be creative is extremely important, as made evident by several decades of research in arts education. The compendium of studies in Deasy demonstrated that it is the active engagement in making art (or music, dance, and drama) that promotes the greatest learning and critical thinking—in and out of the arts.[9] Moreover, it is the sharing of the products resulting from the artistic process, and the confidence that goes along with presenting or performing, that are the most considerable motivators for children in and out of school.[10] Sharing through publishing is also an extremely important component of the literacy process. Intrinsic and extrinsic motivation skyrockets when children have the opportunity to publish and present original work.[11]

A Process Unfolds

At the outset, however, the comic book club at MLKHS was nothing more than a recruiting flyer taped to walls around the school. Participants in the Opening Doors afterschool program chose from a variety of offerings, and in 2004 the comic book club became one of the many voluntary activities. Rebecca had already decided who would be the instructor; she approached one of the school's art teachers, Phil DeJean, who at the time filled in as the afterschool chess club instructor. Phil was not only excited to lead the club but also had an extensive background in and knowledge of comic books, including manga. He named a number of students—all manga fanatics—who were certain to join the club right away. After that, Rebecca and I put the club into Phil's hands, and they were on their way.

The club met every Thursday afternoon from 3:45 to 5:45. It started out with ten teenage boys and girls (six African American and four Latino), then quickly expanded to sixteen (nine African American, six Latino, and one Asian). Phil gave every student a sketchbook in which to jot ideas, characters, dialogue—whatever came to mind. Figure 1.2 is an excerpt from a student's sketchbook.

Phil walked about the room, peering over shoulders, always giving praise, and often making suggestions. As the instructor of this club, Phil was very much a mentor. He rarely lectured; rather, the students came to him for advice regarding character de-

FIGURE 1.2 STUDENT SKETCHBOOK PAGE

sign, panel construction, pencil type, and so on. His typical response was, "What do you think?" Students usually walked away having answered their own questions. Any observer would recognize the level of trust and respect established between this educator and the students. He demanded effort, and they put it forth willingly. The club members seemed reluctant to take a break, and many could be found working on their comic books outside scheduled club hours.

Along with the close relationship they established with Phil, the club members quickly created strong bonds with each other. They critiqued their friends' work, offering helpful hints about the ears on a certain character or the sequence of ideas in a developing section of the story. They also traded manga that they had collected, and they informed the group about new publications and additions to their favorite series. As the club sessions progressed, the group dubbed each other with Japanese nicknames. They began to learn some of the Japanese words that appeared in their favorite manga, words that subsequently made way into the students' own comics: *bishounen* ("beautiful boy"), *mahou shoujo* ("magical girl"), *senshi* ("soldier"). The students practiced lettering in Japanese, and some of the comics incorporated written Japanese phrases.

The sketchbooks soon transformed into storyboards. The students used typing paper and #2 pencils to draft their sequenced panels. Some students worked faster than others, but there was never a race to finish. The pacing of the club was flexible, and a sense of camaraderie rather than competition had been formed. Phil encouraged students to develop their storylines and characters early on, rather than moving ahead quickly and then fixing mistakes later in the process. Once the students had finished a penciled page, they placed it on a lightbox (a tracing mechanism with semiopaque glass and fluorescent bulbs) and employed a variety of black pens to "ink" their work onto a new piece of paper. Phil taught the students how to use the black pens and markers to create shadows and other effects with cross-hatching, a crisscross method common in the comic book medium. The students practiced cross-hatching and other skills in their sketchbooks before applying the techniques to the actual drawings. Soon the pages of dozens of original manga were inked and ready for color.

All of the other comic book clubs that I had worked with to that point had used colored pencils, crayons, or markers to color their comic books. The club at MLKHS did something entirely different. Using flatbed scanners (one of which I donated to the club), they scanned their black-and-white drawings into the old, hulking PC computer in the corner of the room. They then used Adobe Photoshop—specifically the "magic wand" tool—to digitally colorize their artwork. The results were fully designed and colored manga. The students were as amazed as anyone at what they had created. They were proud of themselves, and pleased that other people were so impressed with their work. For many of the club participants, this was the first time that they were celebrated for their accomplishments in school.

Once the club's creations were complete, Rebecca and I worked hard to feature and celebrate the manga in as many ways as possible. With funding secured from TASC, we printed the student work in a full-color publication distributed throughout MLKHS. We arranged a special event at a nearby Barnes & Noble—a store whose managers had often thrown up their hands in exasperation at the students who thronged the manga section after school. The students presented their work to over one hundred people: parents, teachers, friends, and manga enthusiasts. The club members—stars of the event—sat at a big wooden table on a platform with microphones in front of each of them. They introduced their stories, and they spoke about themselves. They explained why manga was so important to them; they discussed their influences and aspirations. The event was covered by a Japanese television station, which brought reporters, cameras, and bright lights. At the end of the panel discussion, we announced the names of two students who had been selected for a summer scholarship donated by the Center for Cartoon Studies in Vermont. The students would travel by train from the steel and concrete of New York City to the trees and rivers of White River Junction to study cartooning for a week. Even I was jealous.

This was the process that unfolded over the course of the first year of the club and that evolved every year thereafter. Many students remained year after year, while new faces came on board and others left as they moved from the school or pursued other activities. There were three reliable figures who laid the groundwork for the club— instructor Phil DeJean, afterschool director Rebecca Fabiano, and Patricia Ayala, a graduate student from Teachers College. I go into more depth about these adults in chapter 5, but suffice it to say that without them the club would not have thrived as it did. The students may have created manga on their own, but they would not have had the opportunity to collaborate with peers, hone their skills, publish their work in print, and become celebrated authors and artists.

Spreading the Word

Much to the surprise of the MLKHS students, their work became a model for other high schoolers across the United States. The spread of their influence began in Chicago with students at Fenger Academy High School, who were involved in CBP through the nonprofit organization After School Matters. This Chicago club had a shaky launch. The twenty-five high school students—all African American boys and girls—who signed up for the club were "apprentices" who each earned $25 per class. They were to spend the semester creating comic books about community engagement, but they had no idea how to begin what quickly seemed an overwhelming task. When I visited, the club was at a standstill. I happened to have some copies of the first MLKHS student publication, which I distributed to the Fenger club members. They proved to be an inspiration. The Chicago students read the New York City comics with great interest, analyzing the characters, backgrounds, and storylines. For some of the Chicago students, the MLKHS comic was their first introduction to manga, and they were instantly hooked. Suddenly, there was a flurry of activity. Desks shifted from the typical classroom rows to stations. Students organized themselves into departments: writing, art, editing, and layout. By the end of the next club session, the students in the Fenger comic book club had a clear plan and were exuberant about the possibilities of what they could accomplish together. And the MLKHS comic book club members had their first fans.

The pool of admirers quickly expanded once the student publications from MLKHS were posted on the CBP website. Three weeks after the first publication was posted, the website's bandwidth exceeded its maximum limit due to, as I frantically discovered, downloads of the MLKHS book. We also received an inordinate amount of e-mail, not from teachers or administrators who wanted to bring CBP to their schools but from children who had downloaded and read the MLKHS comic. They were enjoying the manga from MLKHS alongside their favorite series from Tokyopop and Dark Horse Comics, and they considered the high schoolers experts in the realm of manga. One young admirer from Florida wrote:

> Thank you for the amazing manga! I have some questions for the autors [*sic*]: Is the fox-girl character always both forms or does sometimes she just act like a girl and then become the fox. How did she get her powers? Was it magic or was she born with them? Do her powers ever get her into trouble? How did her little cat get her powers? Why do they eat so much soup? Do you have any advice for me on how to draw manga like you did? Can you PLEASE send me a copy with autograph of the artists!

Educators also became interested in the work of the students at MLKHS, particularly their use of technology. A number of middle and high school teachers involved in CBP were experiencing what one teacher described as "the anticrayon phenomenon." While students took pleasure in writing and drawing original comic books, they viewed coloring as a juvenile activity, something reserved for their bothersome younger siblings. Some teachers sampled computer software such as Plasq's Comic Life, but they found it too constricting, since it offered no opportunity for hand-drawn art.

The teachers found a solution in the precedent set by MLKHS. By scanning their pencil and ink drawings into Adobe Photoshop, the students were able to control the color and layout of every pixel of their work. They experimented with skin tones, size and scale of characters, and a variety of textures in the backgrounds. Teachers in and outside of New York City soon adopted this approach, often using the series of MLKHS publications as a springboard. One high school English teacher soon discovered another benefit of the MLKHS approach—career skill development. Her students became experts in Photoshop; one was awarded a paid summer internship usually reserved for college students because of his mastery of the popular design software. Now the student is in college and majoring in computer science. He plans to develop videogames for cell phones.

Beyond the innovative processes and motivational outcomes of the comic book club at MLKHS, which grew and thrived since that first year in 2004, the content of the student comic books—and the profiles of the students themselves—are worthy of further exploration. For one thing, there are the tangible implications for teaching and learning both in an out of school. But equally important are the social implications. The fact is that most people who are exposed to the comics by the MLKHS students are shocked to learn that almost all of the participating students were African American or Latino. For many, the artwork and writing does not properly align with their preconceived images of the artists. The ensuing questions have become familiar: Who are these kids? Why manga? Do they think they're Japanese? They make these comics in school? Does creating manga help them get better grades? Are they going to do this professionally? Are they aware of how good they are? What do their teachers think about it? What do their parents think about it?

In the next chapters, I delve into these questions and others by analyzing in detail the academic and social impacts of the MLKHS comic book club on the adolescents who participated and the adults who supported them.

Chapter Two

"Superman Is So Silly"

Student Connections to Manga

MORE THAN A FEW FANS—AND FANATICS—of American comic books have been slighted by members of the comic book club at MLKHS. Eager adults, raised on the annals of superheroes-villains, would approach the high schoolers as kindred spirits, assuming comic books would be a common bond between them. As the adult enthusiasts expounded upon their favorite issue of Spider-Man or how the Silver Age of comics was on par with the Golden Age, many of the students rarely held back their scorn. For them, the differences between American and Japanese comics were stark and irreconcilable. Beyond the structure of sequential panels and speech balloons, the two genres were literally and conceptually separated by the Pacific Ocean. Superman was a favorite target of theirs. Back at the school, one female participant said with a smirk, "So this guy is bolting down the street, right towards you, and he's wearing these blue tights and a red cape, and he's bulging all over, know what I mean? I'd be like, 'Call the cops! Get this whack away from me!'" She shook her head, and before turning back to her manga sketchbook, she grumbled, "Superman is so silly."

Exploring Attitudes

Rebuffing the Man of Steel was an attitude shared by many students in the club, particularly the girls. By way of explaining this mind-set, one might presume that the students' disdain for American comics stemmed from one of three overarching issues: gender, race, or age. Such matters have led to the rejection (and rejuvenation) of arts and culture in the past. Regarding gender, the Guerrilla Girls jettisoned the masterpieces of visual art because of gender stereotypes, begging their question: "Do women still have to be naked to get into the Met Museum?"[1] Regarding race, the New Negro movement of the Harlem Renaissance cast off widely held racial stereotypes and forged new art, literature, and music in order to "register the transformations of the inner and outer life" of African Americans.[2] And as for age, teenagers in the 1950s danced right over the music of an older generation when Chuck Berry, Elvis Presley, and Little Richard birthed rock and roll. If these examples demonstrate how gender, race, and age have transformed American society in years past, it is logical to begin with such issues in the investigation of the MLKHS students' embracing of manga over American comics today.

In consideration of gender, classic American comic books are notorious for their portrayal of women as (a) helpless victims waiting to be scooped up by a brawny male superhero, or (b) short-skirted heroines whose special powers are not the only things enhanced by bustiers. As Wright noted, the canon of American comic books was built on "masculine fantasy" where "Superman had little use for women."[3] Wonder Woman, the original female superhero, made her first comic book appearance in 1941 and was introduced as a woman who could take on any problem unsolved by men. Clearly gender stereotyping was not one of those problems, as the men who created Wonder Woman dressed her in a fraction of the clothes worn by her male superhero counterparts. Captain America was covered from head to toe, but Wonder Woman was barely contained in her outfit, presumably because of the warm Mediterranean weather of her island homeland. Her originator, Dr. William Moulton Marston, a psychologist, envisioned the Amazonian superheroine as a role model for young women, but she quickly became a fantasy obsession of the only people who read comic books during World War II—young men.

However, it was not the overcharged sexuality of Wonder Woman or any other female superhero that turned the club members at MLKHS from American comics. In fact, their female manga creations were much more sexually imbued and erotic than Wonder Woman ever dared to be. Created by two girls in the club, figure 2.1 is the cover art for

FIGURE 2.1 STUDENT-CREATED COVER ART FOR AN MLKHS PUBLICATION

an MLKHS publication and features a girl/bat in an extremely short leather dress, nurse's cap, and matching leather collar, armbands, and garters. As in this image, eroticism is a major component of many manga, whether explicit or understated. A particular manga subgenre called *hentai* is extremely pornographic. *Redikomi*, designed for women, and *seijin*, for men, are also sexually uninhibited subgenres of manga. But even conventional manga commonly feature characters with sexual prowess and many with androgynous or transsexual characteristics. The female characters in *shojo* manga universally sport schoolgirl outfits with extra-short skirts that frequently flip high above the upper thigh.[4] As a result of the pervasive sexual ethos of manga, eroticism was something that the MLKHS students incorporated into their own manga characters and storylines without question or concern. As teenagers, sexual development was a fact of life—creating manga was one of their outlets for personal reflection about the role of sex in their lives. Because their work was created in an afterschool setting, the sexual overtones of many of the images went without censorship or repercussion, which they may have incurred in a more formal educational setting.

Did the MLKHS students shun American comics because of racial concerns? Most casual comic book readers would be hard-pressed to identify a nonwhite super-hero throughout the history of American comics. It turns out that there are hundreds, according to the fascinating online collection at the Museum of Black Superheroes.[5] A key reason for the anonymity of these comic book characters is their dodgy past. The first African American comic book figure from Marvel Comics appeared in the 1940s and was named . . . Whitewash. While the rest of his team—the Young Allies—battled the Nazis and other diabolical criminals, Whitewash provided comic relief by inadvertently stumbling into traps, causing the rest of the superheroes an inordinate amount of trouble. In the 1960s and 1970s, the proliferation of superheroes of color resulted from a strange mix of influences from the Civil Rights Movement and blaxploitation—films purposefully stereotyping African Americans. A prime example is DC Comics' first African American superhero named Black Lightning who came to be in 1977. The hero's alter ego was Jefferson Pierce: raised in the ghetto of Metropolis (Superman's hometown), he trained as a successful Olympic athlete and then returned home to become a schoolteacher and an electricity-hurling superhero. On the drawing board, Black Lightning's predecessor was the Black Bomber, a white racist who, when stressed, transformed into a black superhero as a result of chemical experiments during the Vietnam War. The chemicals turned his skin dark for the purpose of camouflage in the jungle. It's little wonder that DC scrapped the Black Bomber for the more palatable, though stereotypical, Black Lightning.

But like questions about gender, racial representation was not the reason why the students at MLKHS turned away from the tradition of American comic books. The students did not seek racially representative characters in the manga they read. They never yearned for, say, a Latino *chibi* ("small child") or an African American *bishounen* ("beautiful boy"). Furthermore, with the exception of some African American samurai warriors developed by boys in the club, the manga the students created abounded with characters that could not look more dissimilar to the youths who spawned them. These magical, whimsical fairies and witches were manga to the core—powdery white skin, oversized eyes and shiny pupils, and silky hair. For as few nonwhite characters that appear in Western-style comics, there are even fewer in manga, and staying true to manga form was important to most of the MLKHS students. Even when the students experimented with new looks for manga characters, such as dark skin tone or dread-locked hair, these characters rarely made it beyond the students' sketchbooks. For the students at MLKHS, it was vital that their manga reflect one thing only—manga itself.

As for age, perhaps the generation of students at MLKHS did not relate to the comics of yesteryear. The current comics market and the movies, television shows, and products are largely based on another generation's superheroes. Most of the comics currently produced by major publishers are continued series from decades ago—the Avengers, Batman, X-Men—or well-timed promotions for upcoming movies. These characters are the foundation of the extensive history of American comics; as long as they continue to draw readers and dollars, the characters will not disappear. As an example, the death of Captain America made national news when Marvel Comics "expired" him in 2007 after a sixty year career of saving citizens of the United States. Steve Rogers, the hero's alter ego, had been on trial for defying a superhero registration mandate and was murdered on the courthouse steps. Interestingly, Superman died for a while in 1992 by the hands of a villain named Doomsday, another cause for media attention. He returned to life seven issues later. Not surprisingly, Captain America was also reincarnated when Bucky Barnes (a sidekick from the 1940s) donned the special costume and shield in 2008. Captain America—the character and the revenue stream—lives on.

However, a generation gap between aging superheroes and today's youth did not account for the shift away from American comics by the MLKHS club participants. Manga has a profound history as well, arguably much deeper than that of American comics. While many point to World War II as the birth of modern manga, when American GIs introduced their comics to Japanese citizens, Adam Kern has identified origins of manga in *kibyoshi*, illustrated picture books that date as far back as the eighteenth century. Frederick Schodt looks back even further to the thirteenth century when Japanese artists created sequential picture scrolls like the *Chojugiga*, a satire on clergy and nobility.[6] Examples of manga precursors such as these are prevalent throughout the history of Japanese art and literature.

Modern manga as we know it today became popular in the 1950s with Osamu Tezuka's character Mighty Atom, branded in the United States as Astro Boy. The design of Astro Boy set the precedent for the style and manner of manga characters, which, like the superheroes of American comics, have remained consistent over the decades that manga has grown and thrived. Unlike American comic book superheroes, however, characters like Astro Boy were relatively short-lived. I would assume that for high school students today a character like Astro Boy might be unfamiliar.

Yet that was not the case at MLKHS. The students embraced the history of manga with enthusiasm. They sought the works of creators who had influenced their favorite manga, and they analyzed the similarities and differences in great detail. Some of the students included in their sketchbooks side-by-side drawings of the same characters with different stylistic inspirations from manga throughout the decades. All around their drawings they scribbled notes to themselves, referring to different artists: "see Takeuchi" or "recheck eyes with Yokoyama." In doing so, they honed their abilities to create manga in a variety of styles, just as dedicated college art students would do in a course of study on figure drawing or lithography. The MLKHS students were aware that, as with American comics, the popular manga titles of today have roots traceable to the past. Rather than turn away from that history, the students aimed to know as much about it as possible. They argued facts with each other related to who influenced whom and to what degree. They made cases for those arguments in the manga itself by flipping to appropriate pages in order to counter a friend's claim for one historical authority over another. The arguments were often loud and passionate, and they could last for several club sessions. However, the disputes were always bolstered by a mutual sense of respect for the subject matter of manga.

Why Manga?

Since inquiries into the topics of gender, race, and age seem to provide insufficient evidence for the preferences and attitudes of the students at MLKHS, the question still remains: Why manga? This is a question I have sought to answer from my very first encounter with students in this comic book club, and a direct question that I assumed would lead to direct and revealing answers. Yet the students' immediate responses to "why manga?" did not match the zeal that characterized their participation in the comic book club. One said, "Manga is cool." Another said, "Masamune Shirow is my idol," without further explanation. Three mumbled, "We just like it." Just as often, students stared at the ceiling in uncomfortable silence. As I discovered throughout the course of this study, the direct question did not lead to comprehensive answers. The students were so close to manga, and had been for so much of their adolescent lives, that explaining their devotion to manga as literature, art, and a lifestyle was unnatural for them. After delivering an in-depth oral thesis on the origins of *shojo* manga or a thorough critique of Nami Akimoto's style in *Miracle Girls*, the students were at a loss for words when asked to consider their own relationships to manga and how it had impacted their lives.[7] They were able to speak about *what* they liked about manga, but they had difficulty putting into words *why* manga was so important to them.

Observations of the students at work and in conversation with each other were more telling. These observations were conducted by Patricia Ayala, the project assistant, and me and via video documentation throughout the club's existence and revealed that, when actively involved in creating or sharing manga, the students freely allowed themselves to express individual ideas and beliefs. In doing so, they explored a range of personal and cultural identities represented by manga. The interview question "why do you like manga?" went unanswered, but analysis of observed interactions of the students—alongside the actual content of their own manga creations—shed some light on why manga excited them to such an extent. A broad picture began to form as to how a distinctly Japanese medium entranced these American high schoolers just as the bastion of American comics became so distasteful to them.

Why manga? One common thread through the students' appreciation for manga is its *lack* of superheroes. The characters in Japanese manga do not wear capes or save the world, although they do often have special magical powers. The character Belldandy from Kosuke Fujishima's *Oh My Goddess!* is a good example.[8] Loosely based on Norse mythology, Belldandy is an employee of the Goddess Relief Agency, along with her sisters Urd and Skuld. Belldandy lands on earth after a male college student named Keiichi accidentally rings the agency's hotline while ordering takeout food. Belldandy grants Keiichi a single wish; on a whim he wishes for Belldandy to remain on earth with him forever. The wish is granted, much to the chagrin of Keiichi, who learns that life with a goddess is not so simple. It turns out that Belldandy has many magical powers: levitation, teleporting, ability to communicate with animals and machines. In fact, Belldandy is so powerful that she must wear a special earring to keep her powers in check. The humor that proliferates in this series, as with so many other manga, is epitomized by the details of Belldandy and her otherworldly sisters. For example, Belldandy can drink alcohol without any inebriating effects, but one sip of soda sends her into a drunken, bubbly rage.

Despite all this, what sets Belldandy most apart from a classic American comic book superhero is that she does not exploit her extraordinary abilities to rescue the world from the grip of an evil villain like the Joker or Lex Luthor. Instead, her sole purpose on earth is to help Keiichi through whimsical events and challenges, ranging from his sister's softball game to a vacation at a haunted hotel. Belldandy does anything she can for Keiichi, no matter how challenging or ridiculous it may seem to him or the reader. This goddess is devoted to an individual rather than the whole of humankind. To that effect, the reader comes to know every detail about Belldandy, Keiichi, and the other characters in this popular series. Readers learn the characters' quirks and tendencies—for instance, that Belldandy is an excellent cook and an even better singer—even though these character traits do not directly relate to a main storyline. Because readers embrace the characters in total, they put faith in them to work through some difficult—and oftentimes silly—situations, thereby allowing the manga authors to experiment with seemingly impossible plot twists. The publisher's brief synopsis of an issue of *Oh My Goddess!* demonstrates the complexity of manga plot:

> Ever since a cosmic phone call brought the literal young goddess Belldandy into college student Keiichi's residence, his personal life has been turned upside-down, sideways, and sometimes even into strange dimensions! When Urd and Skuld are called back to the heavenly realm for remedial training, Belldandy and Keiichi are alone at last! But two things are going to complicate their getting closer as man and woman: Belldandy has come down with a mysterious illness; and, thanks to fooling with Urd's medicine to try and cure her, Keiichi isn't a man anymore—he's a *woman!*[9]

Unwaveringly, the students at MLKHS welcomed a goddess like Belldandy over classic superheroes in their comic books. Superheroes represented for them a two-dimensional life: superhero versus villain with many helpless citizens in between. No matter how dynamic the superhero or interesting the villain, the many people who got caught in the crossfire were faceless and anonymous. Only a few characters truly counted in superhero stories—the hero, villain, a sidekick, and the love interest. The rest were passersby in a superhero's pursuit of justice or a villain's quest for vindication. But these escapist fantasies were completely at odds with the MLKHS students' life experiences. They *were* the people in between. On a given subway ride from her apartment in Brooklyn to MLKHS in Manhattan, a student will experience hundreds of people, each with their own lives, backgrounds, experiences, problems, hopes, fears, and stories to tell. Some have dark skin, others light skin. Some speak Spanish, others English, and others Korean. Some are carrying shopping bags, others tool belts. Some have happy faces, some eyes squint into a crossword puzzle, and others just stare blankly. Some subway riders are going to work; others are homeless. None of these people are represented in superhero comic books. For the MLK students, Superman's skin color was much less of an issue than the fact that he was not human in any meaningful way.

The MLKHS students were straddling the chasm between childhood and adulthood, and superheroes had yet to provide them with any answers to the nagging questions of urban teenage life. Superman did not have to take care of his grandmother after school. Green Lantern did not argue with his brothers about cleaning the bathroom. Wonder Woman did not do laundry. The Hulk did not struggle with algebra. Superheroes did not have to pass the Regents exam in order to graduate high school, or make the decision to go to night school for a GED. Superheroes did not have asthma because of pollution from the endless line of trucks on the Cross Bronx Expressway. Their little brothers did not join gangs and spend years in juvenile justice centers. Superheroes rarely lived with distant relatives; if they did—for example, Peter Parker with his aunt and uncle—it was in Forest Hills or another upscale neighborhood. Superheroes were never able to explain why the MLKHS building contained six different schools, and why a student attended one school instead of another. There were no answers for why weapons got through the school's metal detectors, or why students brought weapons to school in the first place. For the MLKHS students, life was full of confusing details and contradictions that superheroes seemed to gloss over in the effort to battle evil and save the planet.

It was manga's commitment to the mundane and the ordinary that spoke to the students in the club at MLKHS. They enjoyed reading page after page of a conversation between two acquaintances, an exchange that had no more of a point than some simple bonding among friends. In one story, a new transfer student wandered the halls. He was not picked on by bullies, nor did he find new friends. He just wandered alone and ignored. Another plotline featured a girl who daydreamed about being famous, trying on different personalities over the course of a manga. These were the storylines that attracted the students at MLKHS. In turn, the manga that many of the students created concerned daily life experiences. One student's story featured a diner waitress lamenting about her boss. In another a girl and her cat searched for a particularly tasty beef stew. Another featured a boy arguing with his stepparents before he stormed out of the apartment. The very same occurrences happened in the lives of the student manga creators and their friends. Hence, the manga character who struggled in school, sought a new girlfriend, or needed to clean the house came across as sympathetic and representational to the high school club members, even though some of those characters sported fox ears or bat wings.

One student put it best in her critique of a friend's draft of a new manga. The story featured a fairy who would fly above lonely teenagers, tap them on the shoulder, and grant them new and improved love lives. The student criticized the work by saying, "There's too much action here. The fairy should take more time, just talk or do some paperwork or something. This kind of action doesn't happen in real life. Real life is boring." The student critic did not focus on the unreality of a story based on a magical fairy. Rather she criticized the fact that the fairy never stopped to fill out the required forms.

This recognition of and appreciation for the daily grind—subway, school, subway, job, homework, sleep, repeat—kept the students focused on the requirements of making manga over the course of a school year. The process was tedious: character sketches, plot outlines, light pencil drafts, panel designs and layouts, inking, computer finishes. It took the entire year for the most dedicated students to complete a four- or five-page manga. This commitment to their craft impressed outside observers. A representative from TASC who came to observe the MLKHS comic book club was astounded at the number of drafts that the students had produced in working toward a final version to be ready for publication at the end of the school year. She asked the students about their time management and how they were able to accomplish their homework, study for tests, and all the other requirements of school while staying true to their mission of well-crafted manga. One veteran club member, a senior, responded: "This is like a nagging habit, like smoking. But you can't die from this. Well, maybe you can. I know my mom wants to kill me for all the time I spend with manga."

Love Interests

If the incorporation of life's ordinary details addressed the teenagers' sullen side, manga's highlight of love and romance spoke to their, well, teenage side. Many manga feature burgeoning relationships between young people, with a particular focus on the flirtations before a rapport is established. Two characters bound for love often dislike each other at the outset, but a series of mishaps and unforeseen circumstances brings them together. *Love Luck* by Asahina Yuuya is a good example.[10] The story is about a teenage girl named Suzuki Nero, who is ready to declare her amorous feelings for Kurokawa Yamato. But Yamato's annoying twin brother Kurokawa Dan interferes before she gets the chance. In a sudden plot twist, an accident puts both brothers in the hospital. The girl rushes to her love, who unexpectedly kisses her. But wait! It was the wrong brother—the twins have switched bodies in their accident. Unable to revert to their original selves, the boys pretend to be each other when they return to school. This leaves the girl Nero in a true bind. She wants to be with Yamato, which means she has to be with his brother Dan. This is only a sample of the intricacies in this complicated love tale.

The female members of the comic book club at MLKHS found love-oriented plotlines such as this intriguing, and they avidly awaited an author's next contribution to a favorite series. They came to know the characters as companions, and they fervently discussed with other club members the decisions of heroines like Suzuki Nero. The girls also frequented websites dedicated to manga in order to find out about their favorite characters and the authors who created them. One of the most popular sites was Emily's Random Shoujo Manga Page, which is not so random.[11] This site is dedicated to manga specifically intended for girls, and it reviews hundreds of manga by author and theme (i.e., romance, smutty romance, cross-dressing). The blog-style site also includes a page on plot devices in *shojo* manga, which was popular with MLKHS students. Some of the devices are "Obligatory Valentine's Day Story," "Discussions on Park Swings," and "The FIRST KISS!" The students rushed to the sole computer in the classroom in order to check page updates or sneaked into the computer lab in order to get online. They also discovered the speedy Internet connections at Teachers College, where they would peruse multiple manga-related websites while waiting for the scanner to warm up.

Not coincidentally, the MLKHS female students' original manga often incorporated love stories between teens. A manga by Angel—the first student I met at MLKHS—pits a smug boy against the heroine, whose narration describes their mutual revulsion, soon to be love. They call each other nasty names and complain about the other's existence, and yet they continue to keep each other company. An adult reader can imagine the same dance between actual teens, one day despising one another and the next day holding hands. Yet the manga that the female students created seemed to be more a reflection of their interests in manga than their actual love relationships. Whereas real-life relationships might have been just as complex as that of Suzuki Nero and Kurokawa Yamato, they were rarely as humorous. The girls created manga as an artistic passion and literary pursuit, but the light love stories of their own making also seemed to provide a release from the high demands of high school dating, including the all-consuming decision to enter a sexual relationship. The manga developed by these students may have incorporated elements of eroticism in the character designs, but the characters themselves never had physical contact more than a brief kiss. The students certainly pondered the issues of love and sex as their pencils drafted the characters—their poses and placement in the panels of the manga, whether the boy should be physically close to the girl or separated by white space on the page. Rarely did the girls voice these considerations to other club members; the synthesis of thoughts and ideas was contained in their art and writing.

It was not only the girls in the club who sought these soap-operatic love stories in their comic books. Some of the boys read this type of manga as well, and it reflected in the characters and stories that they too created (see chapter 7). The boys' stories that involved emotional relationships tended toward the melodramatic as opposed to the girls' lighthearted romances. Most of the boys' manga, however, did not revolve around love relationships, but instead featured the martial arts and action of the *shonen* manga intended for boys, which I explore in further detail in chapter 4. Yet even these action-oriented comics by the boys incorporated overtones of romance. In one story, the male hero of the story ponders whether or not to release his female lover from an evil spell. Love blinds him, as the woman is transformed into a superhuman demon who kills with a magic sword.

In a few cases, certain MLKHS students fashioned their comic books as a demonstration of an entirely different kind of love, that for a deceased or missing family member. A number of the students had lost family members due to divorce, imprisonment, or death. As a result, many lived with a single parent, grandparents, aunts and uncles, or more distant relatives. The work that some students created in the club represented a type of mourning for those no longer in their lives. A prime example is figure 2.2, created by one of the girls. Her uncle was one of 260 people who died in the crash of American Airlines Flight 587 in 2001. The flight was on its way to the Dominican Republic, deeply affecting the Dominican community in New York. Her

FIGURE 2.2 MOURNING FOR A LOST FAMILY MEMBER

comic book synthesized how she heard about the crash while watching television, the panic in her family, and the confirmation of his death. With this news, the student wrote a tribute to her uncle:

Luisito G. Perreaux was born January 3rd, 1954 in the Dominican Republic, Samana. He was a great man to many people. He had a great business, loving wife and three children. He was also an uncle, brother, son, best friend, and superintendent. He died November 12th, 2001 on Flight 587, and was buried December 2nd, 2001 in "The Gates of Heaven." May he rest in peace.

The comic book continues with preparations for the funeral and a depiction of the lingering sorrow that continues until today. Her story concludes with a close-up of the gravesite and the parting words: "In dedication to my uncle and the passengers of Flight 587. R. I. P."

Whether exploring their everyday lives, future romances, or loves now lost, the students at MLKHS found an outlet for personal creativity and expression in manga. Through the medium, the high schoolers simultaneously celebrated an art form while reflecting on their own personal and cultural identities, which on the surface seemed to have very little in common with Japanese popular literature. But creative art and writing, in this case via original manga, have special ways of breaking stereotypes, enabling a teenage African American girl to express herself through the experiences of a doe-eyed manga character rather than those of Beyonce, Oprah Winfrey, or any other woman of color who might have been a presumed representative of identity. In that vein, the superheroes that so often symbolize the United States as a nation and society missed their mark when it comes to connecting with many of the students in the MLKHS comic book club. Instead the students developed their own heroes in square boxes with limitless borders.

Chapter Three

"I'm Writing for My Life"

Literacy and Learning

FASCINATING AS THE ISSUES of personal and cultural identity discussed in chapter 2 may be, they do not speak to the academic needs of struggling students. Some of the staunchest critics of the American education system—including Gross, Hirsch, Sowell, Stout, and Sykes—bemoan our students' lack of knowledge and inability to read or write as a result of "feel-good" curricula.[1] They contend that schools' promotion of high self-esteem and self-awareness has undercut students' knowledge of important content and learning in general. An English teacher faced with a class of low-performing students and a looming standardized test would be hard-pressed to disagree; the greatest appreciation of "self" and a well-grounded sense of "me" do not help students form compound sentences or write persuasive essays. At first glance, it might seem that the comic book club at MLKHS falls into this curricular trap. After all, the students pursued an element of youth culture that augmented their perceptions of personal identity, helped them build self-esteem, and made them feel good.

And that would be the case, except for the sheer quantity of reading and writing that the club participants consumed and amassed, combined with an improving quality of reading comprehension, spelling, grammar, punctuation, writing mechanics, and other skills. This devotion to words and punctuation after school was all the more intriguing when compared with the students' aversion to these subjects during the school day. In school, the students slogged through Shakespeare and Chaucer. They grappled with verb tenses, vocabulary lists, synonyms, participles, and so on. During the school day, the comic book club members viewed literacy activities as arduous tasks typically resulting in red ink and poor grades. With each passing semester, the tasks became more difficult, and most of the comic book club members struggled to keep pace.

Changing the Context

After school, the students' perceptions of reading and writing transformed dramatically. The MLKHS comic book club members pursued books with anticipation and excitement when the last school bell shrilled. They rushed into the clubroom, mumbled a brief hello to friends from other schools in the building, gave Phil DeJean a peace sign, then got down to work. A variety of manga was strewn across the tables of the clubroom, and students would delve into a chapter of one before jumping to another and then back again. They passed the books around with an approving nod toward one volume and an ambivalent shrug toward another. One student kept a written journal of what happened to her favorite character. Another student silently mouthed the words as he read. On his lap sat a torn paperback dictionary for when he became stumped by a difficult vocabulary word. "Did you read what happened to Naruto?" asked one student, coddling an issue of the popular series by Masashi Kishimoto.[2] His friend responded, "Wait until you read the next chapter. Just wait!"

The students appreciated the artistry and details of the drawings, but the written stories were what truly mesmerized them. At the risk of lagging behind with their own manga work, some students spent hour after hour reading manga in silence as shouts from the hallway and sirens from the street blared. Snack time came with a moan of resentment—students continued reading manga in the hallway, down the stairs, through the chocolate milk and cookies and (untouched) containers of yogurt, and back up to the clubroom, hardly lifting their heads from the books. When the school closed and the students were forced to leave, the club members migrated to the Barnes & Noble up the block on Broadway. They navigated through the well-dressed dinner crowd ready for the ballet at Lincoln Center and the stream of people rushing home from work with shopping bags from Zabar's or Fairway. Up the escalator at the brightly lit bookstore, the students followed a well-trodden path through the aisles to the manga section where they sat, pulled books off the shelves, and read some more.

The students were even more fanatically dedicated to writing. During one club session, a student, nearly out of breath, wrote frantically in a pocket notebook filled with chapter after chapter of his stories. When asked about his work, he responded simply: "I'm writing for my life." The sheer volume of writing was one thing, but the student manga creators agonized over words. They aimed to get the voice of their characters just right without sounding forced or contrived. They strove to capture manga's distinctive literary style, which marries wit, action, and random tangents within the confines of a single panel. The students wrote dialogue and captions that mimicked the manga aesthetic, establishing individual writing styles representative of popular manga creators such as Katsura Hoshino and Tite Kubo. In some cases, the students outlined a plot before forming a draft, but more often their manga grew organically from a picture in a sketchbook combined with written character descriptions. The students developed the stories by reciting prospective plots to friends and soliciting feedback, or by recording their ideas in paragraph form. These various modes of drafting eventually led to the written text that appeared in their comic books. The process was time-consuming and often frustrating, but the students demanded excellence from themselves, in part because they were aware that their work would be read, dissected, and modeled by other manga fans.

As an example of their dedication to the craft of writing, one student spent an entire club session tweaking a single sentence, which at first read: "Then the phantoms go back from the house, and up in the trees." Brow furrowed, the student hovered over the sentence with his pencil and eraser. He scratched out words, rewrote them, and scratched again. He erased the entire sentence and wrote it afresh. He crumpled that paper, tossed it onto the floor, and wrote the sentence again on a clean sheet. The new version read: "Then I watched the phantoms fly back from the house, and up into the trees." He reviewed the wording with the other students at his table and went back to work on the sentence structure. He shared the sentence with Phil DeJean and revised again. Eventually, after much consideration about verb tense, grammatical person, punctuation, and sentence structure, the student wrote: "Then I saw more villains fly from the back of the house and into the trees at blazing speed." Satisfied, he moved to the next sentence out of many that would appear in his comic book.

The logical explanation for this student's dedication to honing a single sentence, after glazing over dozens of paragraphs during English class, is that this was *his* sentence. The comic book that he was creating extended from him—his interests, his ideas, his words. He wanted to make a quality sentence because the words were a part of him and characterized who he was. By way of example, what seemed like a trivial detail in the sentence—the comma—turned into a major conundrum. One of his friends told him that the sentence should not contain a comma because it was not made up of two independent clauses. The boy erased the comma, but the sentence did not look right to him. He read the sentence aloud, once with the comma and once without. He learned from Phil that writers sometimes insert commas in order to indicate a breath, for effect. The student pondered whether he wanted the reader to take a breath in this particular sentence. In the end, the young writer decided to forego the comma; he did not want readers to think that he had made a punctuation error.

Meeting the Standards

When students engage with words, punctuation, and sentence structure in a personally meaningful way as that described above, they are realizing for themselves the value of language and the power of communication—whether in school, after school, or anywhere else. Afterschool educators are very wary of making comparisons between their practices and those of schoolteachers. In the ideal world of an afterschool educator, what transpires after school wholly bolsters the standards and learning that teachers are aiming to instill across school curricula and disciplines. In reality, New York City afterschool programs and the schools in which they are housed are disconnected, with a few rare exceptions. While a school principal may communicate with an afterschool director, the instructors at afterschool programs rarely come into contact with schoolteachers. (Phil DeJean is one of the few schoolteachers who also teaches after school.) As an indication of the distinction between in-school and out-of-school education, New York City schools and afterschool programs are funded and governed by distinct city agencies: schools by the New York State Department of Education and afterschool programs by the Department of Youth and Community Development.

Structure and governance aside, the comic book club at MLKHS is an example of how dichotomous the learning activities can be in school versus after school. A school may choose (or be forced) to use textbooks as the primary teaching tool and multiple-choice exams as the sole mode of evaluation, but an afterschool program could never do so because of a simple but powerful paradox in afterschool education: children are required to learn, but they are not required to attend. How many students would go to MLKHS or any other school in New York City if not forced by parents or guardians?

The city's high school graduation rate is a good indication of an answer—just over 45 percent.[3] Hence, afterschool programs have become very creative in their programmatic offerings, striking a balance between students' interests and the organization's learning goals. Without studying the theories of John Dewey, Maxine Greene, or any other proponent of socially relevant education, afterschool educators have discovered that students can garner knowledge and become dedicated to learning when the subject matter (i.e., manga) is important to the students and the approach (i.e., student-created comic books) is meaningful for them.

The students in the comic book club at MLKHS demonstrated another important yet often overlooked aspect of learning and curricula—creative thinking and academic improvement are not mutually exclusive. In their pursuit of making manga, the club participants met each of the four learning standards in English language arts as mandated by the New York State Department of Education:[4]

- **Standard 1:** Students will read, write, listen, and speak for information and understanding.

- **Standard 2:** Students will read, write, listen, and speak for literary response and expression.

- **Standard 3:** Students will read, write, listen, and speak for critical analysis and evaluation.

- **Standard 4:** Students will read, write, listen, and speak for social interaction.

A closer look at the students' processes and products in creating manga after school highlights just how closely aligned their work was with state standards, unbeknownst to the students and many of the adults in their lives who searched desperately for ways to engage these young people in the core competencies of reading, writing, listening, and speaking.

Standard 1: Students will read, write, listen, and speak for information and understanding.

The club members' entire process of creating manga, from the first sketches to the finished products, revolved around data collection in the broadest sense of the term. They researched and recorded elements of character and storyline from their own work as well as manga by their favorite authors and artists. They took extensive notes as part of this research: "Ears way too big" or "Out of character for Kenji." They notated broad categories of subject matter that they enjoyed reading and liked to pursue in their own manga: "love story," "fight scene," "mother-daughter relationship." Alongside their sketches, the students penned lists of concepts and ideas. Snippets of a story dotted one girl's page with arrows traversing from an idea at the top to another down the side then another at the bottom before cycling back to the top again. The arrows were accompanied by reminders to herself. One arrow was supplemented by the prompt: "Don't go over the top here." Another arrow had a cue in big block letters: "Make it funny!" All of these various modes of data compilation were intended for the students' own reference as they crafted a new manga or banked ideas for future use. Phil DeJean did not instruct the students on how to take notes or summarize plots; the students themselves established this process out of necessity. The enormity of information surrounding the manga that they read and created required self-developed systems of data management.

One example of reading and writing for information and understanding within the context of a student comic book was presented by a longtime club member named Keith (featured in chapter 14). His new story was based in outer space. Whereas another student might have simply designed some planets and described twinkling stars, Keith grabbed a fresh notebook and began to research facts about the universe. He scoured encyclopedia entries, online articles, books, journals, the Tuesday science section of the *New York Times* in search of relevant information for his comic book. The first page of the notebook featured the names of the planets in our solar system along with their dimensions, volumes, temperatures, atmospheric contents, and distances from the sun. On the second page, he sketched each of the planets twice, once with a view from far away and once in close-up perspective. On page three, he wrote facts about how the universe was formed, and he drew his own visual interpretation of the Big Bang. Over the course of a month, Keith's notebook became an astronomer's log of outer space, full of handwritten details about the possibility of life on Mars and arguments for and against Pluto as a planet. By the time Keith was ready to begin his comic book, he had taught himself about the entire planetary system.

Keith read and wrote for information and understanding, but he also listened to and spoke about data, concepts, ideas, and theories. He enthusiastically sought opportunities to speak with others about his newfound knowledge. Notebook under his arm, Keith became the resident expert on astrological science. If a fellow student needed to know which planet a samurai warrior should visit in order to break from an evil ice spell, Keith was certainly the person to ask. When I inquired about the new comic book that he was developing, Keith answered by asking me in return, "Do you know which planet is the heaviest? Jupiter. But guess what? Jupiter is made of gas, mostly hydrogen and helium. Isn't that amazing?"

Aside from gathering and communicating information and understanding related to content, the MLKHS comic book club members accomplished a substantial amount of reading, writing, listening, and speaking about manga as an entity and its country of origin, Japan. Of course, the students read manga, and they wrote in the process of creating their own comics. But they also read extensively *about* manga—its history, influences, creators, and literary modes. The sources for this information were varied, ranging from magazines to websites to books to museums. One information source was a 2007 issue of *Wired* magazine titled "Manga Conquers America," with a number of articles devoted to manga as an art form, business, and cultural phenomenon.[5] Of particular interest to the students was an article by Daniel Pink, which contrasted the worldwide success of manga with the sagging sales of printed manga in Japan.[6] The article stated that the Japanese were not turning away from manga; they were getting their manga via cell phones instead of books.

This information fascinated the MLKHS students. They listened to each other's take on the cell-phone phenomenon in Japan and spoke to one another about the details. One student thought that manga on cell phones would be a great way for more people to access the stories. Another student thought that this electronic medium would destroy manga entirely, and she nearly cried to think about it. After heated discussions, the students wrote on blogs, e-mail messages, and text messages about how this new trend in manga might affect them and the future of their prized art and writing. In short, the students acquired, interpreted, applied, and transmitted information; they also demonstrated understanding through reading, writing, listening, and speaking. Although these unique and unconventional approaches to acquiring information and building understanding rarely surface in English language arts classes, the students' processes were very much in tune with the first literacy standard as mandated by the New York State Board of Regents.

Standard 2: *Students will read, write, listen, and speak for literary response and expression.*

It should be evident by now that the club participants at MLKHS treasured manga. They embraced it as writing and art. They cherished the stories and followed the lives of the characters, and were well versed in the backgrounds of their favorite authors. They analyzed the forms, structures, and contents of the narratives, and they reflected and expounded on these literary constructs. As a synthesis of their thoughts and observations, the students' written works echoed influences of culture, society, upbringing, and individual perspective. Certainly, literary theorists and critics peering into the literary lives of these adolescents would be likely to conclude that these youths had discovered for themselves the true nature of literary pursuit: the MLKHS students used written words and visual imagery as a dual pathway to personal enjoyment and the expression of values.

Yet from the students' vantage point, their favorite books and their written works seemed as far as imaginable from the accepted canon of literature. Manga did not appear on their reading lists. The Regents did not ask questions about classic manga. Manga was not mentioned in the required compendium of literature that the students were handed each year. Although manga had become a mainstay of youth culture, the categorization of manga as serious literature for a high school audience had certainly not been realized in the classrooms of MLKHS. Several students reported teachers who banned manga in class because of the genre's reputation for adult content or its sapping of the students' time and energy from the books that they were required to read in school. Most of the students' parents or guardians held the same negative view of manga. The guardians of at least two students forbade their participation in the club because manga seemed to supersede homework. At one culminating exhibit of the MLKHS comic books, a grandparent said to me about her grandson: "I really wish he wouldn't do any of this comics stuff, but I'm just tired of arguing." Unbeknownst to them, many of these adult figures made appearances as characters in the student comic books. Needless to say, the students got revenge.

Regardless of how adults in the students' lives viewed manga, the students themselves were unconditionally committed to manga as literature. They summarized and analyzed plots on a regular basis, paying special attention to imagery and recurring themes. They distinguished distinct literary subgenres of manga, such as *shojo* designed for girls, *shonen* marketed to boys, and *kodomo* for very young children. They documented and paraphrased sources about manga, which established an understanding of why and how the books were written. The students explored and considered the broader historical, societal, and cultural contexts surrounding manga, and how those forces impacted storylines, series development, publication trends, and the authors who wrote the books.

This deep appreciation for books and written language was accompanied by an ongoing consideration of how manga texts related to the students' own lives. Personal reflection such as this transpired in a number of ways. The club members at MLKHS considered the decisions of the characters in their favorite manga and how they themselves would have acted in a similar situation. For example, in *Hayate, the Combat Butler* by Kenjiro Hata, the main character is a teenager named Ayasaki Hayate, abandoned by his parents who have amassed an enormous gambling debt.[7] Now gangsters are after Hayate to settle the score. The club members put themselves in the role of Hayate, asking questions such as: "Would I forgive my parents for putting me in this situation?" "Would it be OK to use violence to protect myself from the gangsters?" "If I could get the money back without getting caught, would I keep it?" The students also synthesized the relationships between literature and life by creating original manga reflective of the works that they had read. If a manga introduced a troubled relationship between two best friends, the students spoke about and listened to each other's views on the dilemma, but they also incorporated the theme of strained relationships into a new original manga. They published and shared those new works with other club members and a community of manga readers at large, thereby adding to this literature that they had adopted as their own.

Standard 3: *Students will read, write, listen, and speak for critical analysis and evaluation.*

The participants in the comic book club approached manga with a critical eye. The students intensely analyzed the content of the books, especially the storylines. Given the volume of manga produced by so many publishers, the students were able to quickly recognize subpar art and writing. In one particular manga, for example, the students were upset about the author's use of a dream sequence. They felt that the plot twist was a "cop-out." Where the author could have attempted strong conflicts and resolutions within the story, he opted instead for an easy way to introduce new characters. The students shared criticisms such as this with each other, warning friends about weak narratives and recommending must-reads. Of course, the students did not always agree with each other. In the process of arguing about the attributes of one manga versus another, the students accomplished a good amount of speaking and as much listening as a vociferous argument would allow.

I experienced the full force of the students' evaluative abilities when I pulled together an informal focus group to examine a series of books that I was asked to review. A publisher produced *Shakespeare: The Manga Edition*—manga versions of *Hamlet*, *Julius Caesar*, *Romeo and Juliet*, and *Macbeth*.[8] I had a sense that the books were not representative of manga as an art form. Unsure, I asked some students at MLKHS to scrutinize the books. They were furious. "It's NOT manga!" they shouted at me as though I were responsible. "Manga is supposed to be whimsical!"; "Just because the characters have big eyes, does not make it manga"; "Manga is supposed to read quickly and not get bogged down in so much text." Their consensus was that the publisher had stuck the buzzword "manga" on the cover to increase sales. "A real Shakespeare manga would go like this," said a female student—she drew Romeo as a *bishounen* in a sharp suit and Juliet as a *shoujo* (girl) with the ears and tail of a red fox.

The students were skilled critics of their own work and that of peers. They self-evaluated their manga each step in the creative process. Their sketchbooks demonstrated multiple drawings of the same character, which seemed logical for an art-oriented project. But the sketchbooks also contained numerous versions of written dialogue and captions. One student wrote a sentence four different ways: one with an opening clause, another as a compound sentence, the third as a phrase and parentheses, and the last as two clauses separated with a dash. To the right of each sentence the student placed a checkmark by her favorite and an "x" by the others. The self-evaluations continued as the comics developed. Some students designed their panel layouts and photocopied those pages in order to write and draw several versions of the same page. Once drafted, the versions were compared, and the students selected the one that made the best addition to the manga.

Peer evaluation was another important aspect of the club's process. Sometimes this communication was informal—a glance over a friend's shoulder and a word of encouragement. The praise was often specific to a particular character design, the appearance of a speech bubble, or the way a word was written. The note of admiration was quick and unobtrusive, especially as club members worked around a table. When praise was offered, it was often returned. One student responded to a friend's praise by saying, "Thanks, and I like what you did with the teacher character in yours. It's great!" On the other hand, the evaluation from peers was not always positive. Club members could be seemingly brutal in appraising a friend's work, especially if they knew that the person could do better. They rarely held back criticism if they believed it was warranted. Surprising to me, this type of critique was always taken well. Rather than turning to tears or arguing about the condemnation, the student in question simply crumpled the paper and tossed it in the garbage or folded it into a sketchbook for future reference.

Standard 4: *Students will read, write, listen, and speak for social interaction.*

Collaboration was a mainstay of the MLKHS comic book club. While most of the student-created comic books originated from an individual, the students aided each other with certain aspects of the process. One student showed a predilection for and interest in inking (applying thin black markers to outline the pencil drawings of a comic book and incorporate shading). Although it might seem a straightforward task, inking requires many critical decisions that affect the overall tone and atmosphere of a comic book. By way of example, comic book artist Gary Martin inked thirty-six versions of the same image with different shadows and techniques, and each one appeared remarkably different.[9] At MLKHS, one particular student became an in-house inker for some of the other club participants, thereby honing his specialized skill and allowing the rest of the club members to focus on their drawing techniques and storylines. Other students interested in technology scanned and colored the inked art. The inkers and color specialists consulted with the original artists and writers, and together they made decisions about the design of the finished product.

Regarding the conventional literacy competencies of reading, writing, listening, and speaking, the MLKHS club members not only honed these skills by creating manga but also created manga for the very purpose of exercising these skills as a social pursuit. It is safe to say that many of the students in club would have created manga on their own. Yet they chose to participate in the club so that they could read each other's work, write comments in the margins, listen to new ideas about manga, and speak their own opinions. Often the noise became earsplitting, eliciting a "shush" from Phil. The volume decreased to a normal conversational level, began to rise with the introduction of a new character in one student's manga, developed to shout level as friends got excited about something the character said, became deafening as the whole club joined in, and then "shush" again.

This scenario is familiar to any teacher, but it is important to remember that the subject of all this chatter was neither *American Idol* nor a high score in *Grand Theft Auto*. These adolescents forged a connection through manga that fostered discussion not only about books, writing, and art but also many things outside of the texts. These dialogues often took place while the students worked on their original manga. I witnessed a very deep discussion between two students who, in the process of talking about the influence of race in the presidential election, never looked up from their papers and whose pencils continually danced across their pages. For them, manga became a literary pursuit and an opportunity to delve into important life issues. One could expect nothing more from literature.

Chapter Four

"My Name Is Sayuri"

Identity and Culture

THERE WERE MANY TANGIBLE CONNECTIONS between literacy and identity in the MLKHS clubroom, but they did not all come in the form of English language arts. Japanese culture and language were deep-rooted in the lives of these urban American high schoolers. Manga was not only a pathway to literacy for the club members but also a window into another place and a people thousands of miles away. The students' connection to Japan was remarkable, considering that Japanese society could not be more dissimilar to the neighborhoods where the MLKHS students lived. Japan is homogeneous; New York City is heterogeneous with people from many different backgrounds and countries of origin living within close proximity. Japan is predominantly monolingual; the 2000 census report of one neighborhood in New York City identified more than 30 languages spoken by residents and fewer than 20 percent of households with English as the sole language.[1] While Japan has certainly had its economic hardships, it does not boast the stark contrast between the astronomically rich and the devastatingly poor so evident in New York City. The MLKHS students fell into the latter category—schools in the building received federal Title I funding with a high percentage of eligibility, according to the New York City Department of Education.[2]

Despite these disparities, the MLKHS students cherished everything Japanese. They discussed Japanese fashion, technology, and cultural trends. Two girls mapped out a trip to Tokyo—where they would visit, the stores they would patronize, the noodles they would slurp, how they would ride the *shinkansen* (bullet train). This trip was obviously a fantasy, as the one detail that the girls overlooked was how they would pay for the tour. Unable to visit Japan, some of the students scrutinized published manga for hints about Japan, ranging from the height of Mount Fuji to the taste of sake. Rather than researching dry facts and details in an encyclopedia (or more likely Wikipedia), the students attempted to understand how Japan fit into the context of manga—not vice-versa as cultural critics or anthropologists might aim to demonstrate. Manga was the students' entry point into Japan. Without manga, it is safe to assume that the students would have shown as much interest in Japan as they did Russia, Bolivia, or Canada—which was very little.

In some respects, the students' bond with Japan was reflected in a memoir and travelogue titled *Wrong About Japan* by Peter Carey.[3] Because of his preteen son's engrossment with manga and anime, Carey and his son Charley traveled to Japan in order to experience the manga motherland. To Carey's dismay, Charley showed little interest in witnessing or learning about traditional Japanese culture (i.e., calligraphy, kimonos, *ikebana* flower arranging). The boy's only desire was to visit boisterous manga and anime shops and to meet famous creators such as Hayao Miyazaki, best known for the animated film *Spirited Away*.[4] Throughout the trip Carey tried to frame manga and anime within his own Western-bred perceptions of Japanese history and culture, but his interpretations were often proved wrong by his son and their teenage guide Takashi. Like Charley, and in many ways Takashi, the MLKHS students equated manga with *their* Japan, not the Japan of history primers or social studies textbooks. It was a colorful, fast-paced, high-tech Japan centered around cute and whimsical manga characters, not serene teahouses or ancient Buddhist temples.

Then again, the MLKHS students did strive to learn about aspects of Japanese history and traditional culture as long as those things correlated with manga. For example, in 2006 the manga scholar Masami Toku brought her worldwide traveling exhibit of historic *shojo* manga to the Pratt Institute in Brooklyn, a show that I helped to facilitate and organize. The exhibit featured twenty-three renowned *shojo* manga creators and more than two hundred works from World War II to the present. Among the attendees from the Japanese Consulate, the Japan Foundation, and the Japan Society were students from MLKHS. They weaved through the suited gentleman and stood close to the original works hanging on the wall. Reading the labels and examining the manga, the students learned about the cultural consequences of World War II, the role of women in Japanese society, and the importance of visual imagery in Japanese culture. They came away with a new appreciation for manga as an historic art form and Japan as a country with a fascinating and unique culture.

Learning the Language

The manga that the MLKHS club participants read was translated into English from the original Japanese, but the books retained plenty of Japanese words and phrases. In some manga, the translators kept storefront signs or menu items in Japanese for authenticity's sake, not to mention the difficulty and expense of redesigning these things in English. As a result, many of the MLKHS students were learning to read, write, and speak some Japanese. Just as they would in reading English, the club members made inferences about the meaning of a written Japanese word via the word's context in a manga. A word such as *dashi* that appeared in a market scene likely referenced foods or goods. When the character complained about a pot of hot *dashi* that spilled and scalded him, the students inferred that *dashi* was cooked in a pot and could easily spill, like soup. Japanese letters that appeared on the front of a bus likely referenced a city or destination. If the English caption in the comic book panel referred to Tokyo, the students were able to match the Japanese and English written forms, and they recognized the Japanese word in future manga. Other Japanese words that the students read were generally specific to manga. For example, *bishoujo* translated to "beautiful girl" and *bishounen* to "beautiful boy." These words often appeared in the context of manga, and the students easily recognized such vocabulary through repetition in the many books that they consumed.

Some students practiced Japanese lettering in their sketchbooks in a manner akin to traditional calligraphy, drawing individual strokes several times over. They attempted to achieve a perfectly consistent look to each stroke, adjusting arm position or angle of the pen until the simple images appeared fluid and unencumbered. After much practice, they appreciated the importance of relaxation as a key to good Japanese lettering; too tight a handgrip or an unfocused mind led to unwanted variation in the lines. The single strokes graduated into line series, which then transformed into words. The students who wrote Japanese in this way often copied the letters from a manga, just as apprentices of calligraphy carefully reproduce the work of a master calligrapher. Sometimes the students were aware of the meanings of the words they wrote; other times the tantalizing appearance of the letters inspired the detailed writing process. This form of artistic lettering was synchronized with the students' artistic energies, and it allowed them to consider words in the context of creative processes. They spoke of "drawing" Japanese letters rather than "writing" them, and they often intertwined the letters with pictorial images for their manga. Figure 4.1 is an example of some Japanese writing from a female club member's comic book.

The MLKHS students also spoke some Japanese, again words and phrases that they had gleaned from manga. Some club members greeted their friends by saying *konnichiwa* ("good day") and departed with *sayonara* ("goodbye"). Some answered questions with *hai* ("yes") or *iie* ("no"). One girl tapped her friend on the shoulder and said, "*Sumi masen*" ("excuse me"). Once she obtained the pen she needed, she said, "*Domo arigato*" ("thank you"). Many of the club participants dubbed themselves with Japanese nicknames by which they called one another. One girl whom I addressed by

FIGURE 4.1 EXAMPLE OF JAPANESE WRITING FROM A CLUB MEMBER'S COMIC

her given name wagged her finger at me and said, "Uh-uh. My name is Sayuri. Or should I say, '*Watashi no namae wa Sayuri desu.*'" With their new names intact, the students occasionally tested each other on Japanese vocabulary when they gathered around the clubroom and drew manga. One student asked her friend to provide the Japanese word for "water." The friend did not know the answer; he said instead, "*Gomen nasai,*" meaning "I am sorry."

Mangaka High

Despite increasing opportunities for women in Japan's businesses, government entities, and educational institutions, many Japanese women maintain traditional lives defined by childcare and homekeeping rather than moneymaking careers.[5] In the world of manga, however, women often run the show. Female characters play consistently important roles in manga stories, and they are often strong-willed, exceptionally skilled, and extremely smart. More importantly, manga is often created by women. Although manga designed for girls was originally created by men, many *mangaka* (manga creators) in Japan today are women. According to Toku, manga by female *mangaka* first gained ground in the 1950s.[6] Some of the pioneering women in the field are Masako Watanabe, Miyako Maki, and Hideko Mizuno—all born before 1940. Their work led to the advancement of *shojo* manga for girls, which has grown to become one of the most widely distributed subgenres of the manga market.

The girls in the MLKHS club identified with Japanese women *mangaka*. The students respected what these women had accomplished as artists and business leaders. They followed the women's work intently, proud that some of their favorite manga was created by the very same people for whom it was intended: females. One of the girls in the club was especially reverential of Machiko Hasegawa, the first successful female *mangaka*. Born in 1920, Hasegawa began as a manga assistant in the 1940s, but she developed her own character and series titled *Sazae-san*, which was published for nearly thirty years.[7] *Sazae-san* featured the life of a modern Japanese woman and her family; it spawned an anime series that is still in production today, making it the longest-running animated television series in the world. The MLKHS girls who researched Hasegawa's life and work understood how difficult it must have been for her to break into a field dominated entirely by men. The life of someone like Machiko Hasegawa inspired some of the girls to pursue their passions in the workforce no matter what obstacles might arise.

The Japanese women *mangaka* who most epitomized the girls in the MLKHS comic book club were collectively known as CLAMP. Originally launched in 1989, CLAMP was founded by twelve women led by Ageha Ohkawa, formerly known as Nanase Ohkawa. Like the girls at MLKHS with their Japanese nicknames, the members of CLAMP have "tried on" different names to suit their evolving interests and personalities. More to the point, however, the large body of work that CLAMP produced over the decades crossed stylistic boundaries. Their work was not intended for girls alone but reached readers of both sexes, across age ranges, and over international borders. The result was an enormous cult-like following and sales near 100 million copies. Similarly, the MLKHS girls strove to create manga that was interesting and important to them rather than works that would be pigeonholed as a certain genre or for a specific audience. CLAMP was a model for the female club members as to how women could work together in support of each other while maintaining individual voices and styles within the context of manga. The independent streaks in both CLAMP and the MLKHS girls represented the commitment of these women to stay true to their ideals while forging their own ways within the realms of the creative arts and business.

Way of the High School Samurai

While the female club members at MLKHS connected with Japan through female-centric stories and the women *mangaka* who created them, the male club members cultivated a link to Japan with one of that nation's most revered and storied facets: the samurai warrior. Their work was a blend of *shonen* manga (action-oriented comics usually featuring male protagonists) and the various Asian martial arts that have dotted the landscape of American popular culture for decades. Many of the youths had been introduced to the martial arts of East Asia, including the samurai code, by way of the rap goup Wu-Tang Clan, the influential movie *Ghost Dog: The Way of the Samurai*, several popular video game titles, and a number of anime shows.[8] While these sources certainly warped the historical accuracy of the samurai, they did introduce the students to an admirable social credo translated from the eight virtues of the samurai *bushido*, including justice and honesty, sympathy toward all people, and politeness. These doctrines were furthered in some of the samurai-oriented manga that the boys enjoyed reading, especially *Lone Wolf and Cub* by Kazuo Koike and Goseki Kojima and *Rurouni Kenshin* by Nobuhiro Watsuki.[9]

Of course, violence is a fact of samurai life, and one cannot discount graphic blood-shed as a reason for the boys' attraction to the samurai tradition in Japan. The boys' original manga featured systematic training regimens of samurai warriors who used ultrapowered punches and a variety of swords and other weapons to defeat sparring partners, villains, and monsters. The samurai fighters faced numerous personal and physical challenges, but they always prevailed. With each new trial, the characters gained wisdom and physical strength, along with a new cache of weapons, which they used to further their status as warriors and men. In numerous cases, a young novice fighter grappled with his personal limits at the merciless hand of a tutor. The fierce tests would certainly have killed anyone other than a comic book character, but they served to help the warrior find strengths in ways that overcame his shortcomings. In the end, the trainee combated and eventually defeated his proud though beaten and bloody master.

Much can be inferred from the MLKHS boys' affinity for the Japanese samurai. On one level, the samurai established a strong work ethic and were rewarded for being diligent. The boys at MLKHS put a great amount of effort into creating manga, which was self-rewarding as they relished this process and the tangible products that resulted. But the boys also worked hard at school, and that had proved unrewarding for many of them. Despite homework help and tutoring provided by the afterschool program, required remedial classes, and a continuous barrage of test preparation, many of the boys struggled academically and had done so for most of their school years. Some were dangerously close to dropping out. Fortunately, the Opening Doors afterschool program encouraged the struggling students to forge on, in part by keeping the students in the building through offerings like the comic book club. For these male adolescents, the samurai warriors imparted hope that their efforts in school would one day be rewarded with a diploma. Graduation day was something like the final battle of a samurai tale; after all the grades and test scores were tallied, the students were ushered through, scarred and bandaged but ready for the next phase in life.

On another level, the samurai found a way to organize, in fact systematize, violence. Samurai warriors followed a training agenda, and some of their battles were scheduled events in a series of ongoing proceedings. Samurai fighting was enshrouded in honor—each samurai respected his opponent and strove to be merciful and just. This predictable organization of violent occurrences was a severe contrast to the random violence in the lives of many of the MLKHS boys. Along with what may have happened at home or on the street, the list of violent incidents at MLKHS itself over the years was a long one. In 2002, two boys were shot inside the school. In 1997, six students were charged with sexually assaulting a thirteen-year-old girl in a bathroom. In 1992, a gang attacked two students with a pipe and a machete outside the building. In 1990, a fifteen-year-old student was shot in the stomach by another student inside the school. More recently, data in the New York State Department of Education Violent and Disruptive Incidents Report for 2005–06 documented violence in the building ranging from "reckless endangerment with weapons" to "serious physical assault without weapons."[10] These were merely the reported cases of school violence, far fewer than the actual incidents, according to the city comptroller.[11]

The MLKHS boys did not expect an end to violence. As they walked through the school metal detector every morning and woke to gunshots at night, violence was a given—a fact of living in their particular neighborhoods and in this particular school building. Rather, these African American and Latino teens created samurai-oriented manga in part to put a face of order on the randomness of violence and the constant fear it generated. The samurai trials—that is, knowing the face of your enemy and when he will attack—balanced the insecurity of what awaited anyone rounding a corner or entering the stairwell at school. The knowable honor and respect required of a samurai battle counteracted the haphazard nature of gunfire or the sudden chaos of a gang attack. Ending violence was not an option for the MLKHS boys; making sense of violence was the best they could do.

The boys who created samurai-driven manga broke ranks with other students in the club by developing characters that resembled the teenagers themselves. For example, the samurai in figure 4.2 is named Ryu—age 14—an African American warrior. As the first panel of the comic book reads: "His only desire is to learn, but people in his village stood in his way. Now he chooses to fight and make that his career . . ." The congruence to the author's life and his neighborhood is not difficult to trace. For this manga creator and other boys in the group, staying true to a traditional manga character set was less important than developing original depictions that were personally valuable to the boys who created them. By incorporating representative characters into their comics, the boys *became* the story rather than creators distanced from the page. They lived the lives of the characters, empowering the samurai, and therefore themselves, to control the words, actions, decisions, and, of course, the violence. Ryu won in the end, not because he sported superpowers or outwitted his enemies, but because he had control.

FIGURE 4.2 SAMURAI EXPLOITS BY A MALE CLUB MEMBER

Publish and Prosper

Whether it was the girls creating *shojo* manga or the boys designing samurai characters, all of the students in the club connected with Japan and its manga readers on one fundamental level: *doujinshi*, or self-published work, and it applies to thousands of fans in Japan who create manga for fun and as a celebration of the literary form. Japan boasts large conventions for *doujinshi* creators to meet each other, swap original manga, and discuss practices and techniques. The largest convention, known as Comiket, meets in Tokyo twice a year and draws over a half-million attendees.[12] The explosion of *doujinshi* is fueled by the Japanese insatiability for manga—publishers cannot product it fast enough. Therefore, fans take to the pen (or increasingly the computer) to design their own stories and characters. Oftentimes their work is a derivative of professionally published manga; sometimes fans simply utilize well-known characters and continue storylines from their favorite manga. Some of Japan's most renowned *mangaka*—including CLAMP—began their careers as amateur *doujinshi* makers. Furthermore, many professionals in the field return to their *doujinshi* roots to build excitement about new works and introduce fresh characters into the rapidly flowing stream of published manga.

There are some parallels to *doujinshi* in the United States. For example, "fandom" is the practice of writing and communicating, often online, about books, music, and other media. Donna Alvermann and Margaret Hagood examined case studies of music fandom and the extensive conventional and new literacy skills involved in the process of writing about a favorite band or song.[13] Kelly Chandler-Olcott investigated the role of the Internet in fandom specific to manga and anime, and the building of multimodal literacies.[14] Her research touched on the many Internet sites dedicated to manga fandom, almost all with blogging opportunities for fans to cheer their favorite manga and jeer their most despised. Perhaps more akin to *doujinshi* is "fanfiction," where fans write continuations of their favorite books and stories, including manga. Fanfiction was born well before the Internet age with fans of *Star Trek* building on television scripts to write new stories about Mr. Spock and Captain Kirk. Today, however, fans write extensions to all kinds of stories, including the classics, as with the story about Romeo and Juliet's parents by a writer who goes by jigokushoujo01 on www.fanfiction.net.[15] Rebecca Black researched the literacy implications of fanfiction for English language learners whose stories enabled them to reach a broad audience of readers and access multiple community writing resources.[16] Finally, the production of "zines" (short for "fanzines") is another literary practice that is close to *doujinshi*. Barbara Guzzetti and Margaret Gamboa investigated girls' use of zines to advocate for social justice and in the process create original essays and artwork on their own time and with their own resources.[17]

Although the practices at MLKHS had similarities to other literary pursuits like fandom, fanfiction, and zines, they were more akin to Japanese *doujinshi*. The students in the club prized the opportunity to publish manga. Although they found the process of creating manga fulfilling, it was publishing their work (and meeting the deadlines inherent therein) that moved the students from their sketchbooks to penciled drafts to finished works. Beginning in 2005, the club produced a printed collection of student comics at the end of each school year. TASC funded the first publication. Printing costs were subsequently divided between the Opening Doors program and the Comic Book Project. Acceptance into the publication did not come easy for the participants. They needed to commit to the club for the entire academic year, not just because of the attendance requirement but also because frequent absences equated to an incomplete comic book ill-suited for publication. Some students who joined the club at the beginning of the year disappeared after the first week or two when the realities of the time commitment became clear. The students who took on the responsibilities of the club formed something of a *doujinshi* circle—a group of like-minded individuals who supported each other in their efforts to create and eventually publish manga.

The distribution of the culminating publication was a major event at the after-school program. Months of exertion, usually compounded in the final weeks before the deadline, finally revealed their significance as the program director tore open the shipping boxes and extracted the shiny, colorful books. The students delicately handled the printed pages, deciding which cover to examine first—the front cover for the stories that read left to right or the "other front cover" for the manga that read right to left. Upon first opening the books, they flipped directly to their own stories and read with intense concentration as though seeing them for the first time. They ran their fingers over the characters and smiled, clearly proud that this product resulted from their efforts. Then the club members located their friends' work, and the silence was shattered by laughs and congratulatory expressions. "You snuck it in! You snuck it in!" one girl hollered at her friend. We will never know their private joke, but for them it meant the world to see it in print. For almost all of the club members, these books represented the first printing of their work and the first time that their achievements of art and writing had been featured. The celebratory nature of "distribution day" was emotional for both the students and the adults.

As in Japan, the publishing of the one's comics was both a pastime and a business for some of the MLKHS students. As a rule, they did not sell the end-of-year publications, but some students did use the books as examples of their work for profitable purposes. Samantha (featured in chapter 9), a veteran member of the club, created a flyer that offered her services in designing custom *chibis*, or small, childlike characters. On the flyer, Samantha distinguished between detailed designs (three dollars) and less-detailed drawings (two dollars), color versus line drawings, and a single character versus multiple versions. She also offered "regular" manga characters, head and shoulders, down to the waist, or a full-body design. Samantha took requests, but "no extremely graphic requests, please." And, of course, all prices were negotiable. At the bottom of the flyer she listed her contact information for e-mail and instant messaging, and she provided the addresses for her blog and MySpace page. She even established a PayPal account in order to accept online payments. Just as *doujinshi* specialists who offer their services to help others create original characters, this student found a way to turn her passion for manga into money, and she did not hesitate to capitalize.

The connection to Japanese *doujinshi* was furthered at MLKHS with the respect that the participating students gained from their publications. The top *doujinshi* creators in Japan are treated like royalty at events like Comiket. Fans rush to scoop up rare copies of limited works, and they trade their comics commodities in order to obtain desired rare titles. The group of students who started in the club as confirmed outsiders with a seemingly strange passion for Japanese manga, ended up publishing works that drew admiration from other students in the afterschool program. Curious friends and other nonmembers hovered around the clubroom to witness the mastery of the most skilled artists in the club. They wanted to know about how the comics were developed and why the club participants spent so much time at their craft. They flipped through sketchbooks of the club members, pointing to images and shaking their heads in disbelief at the artistry of what the students had created with regular pencils and blank paper. In return, many of the club members realized increased self-confidence in their skills as artists, writers, and important constituents of the after-school community.

Manga Psyche

There are several theories as to why Japanese citizens have been and continue to be so attracted to manga. Takashi Murakami argued that the aftershocks of World War II, especially the dropping of atomic bombs on Hiroshima and Nagasaki, scarred the Japanese psyche, resulting in an escapist desire for cute and innocuous characters and plotlines.[18] It is hard to imagine how the club participant who was homeless or the one who was abused by her parents were not also scarred by their difficult life experiences. Their investment in happy, sweet characters may have matched the Japanese desire to block the hurtful events from the past or, in fact, the present. Here was an opportunity to step into another life, whether it was the fantastical whims of a *shojo* schoolgirl or the invincible powers of a samurai warrior. The experience of creating manga provided some of the students with a pathway for creative and personal expression that might have otherwise seemed impossible. In this way, manga became art therapy.

In another theory, Brent Wilson argued that manga is representative of Japan's tremendous need for ingenuity, creativity, and imagination. He wrote: "Japan is a country whose very survival . . . depends on the development of the one natural resource it has in abundance, the minds of its young people."[19] This theory, too, could be applied to the context of the comic book club at MLKHS. The participants discovered one resource in their lives that no one could take away or destroy: the power of their own creativity. This was not an insignificant resource. By creating original manga and publishing their work for a larger audience, the student club members mined their creativity for self-confidence, respect, and in some cases monetary reward. Had they been born in Japan, their creativity might have been praised alongside that of the most prominent *doujinshi*. At MLKHS, though, the club members could only imagine a place and people thousands of miles away who would embrace such creativity as an asset, one to be celebrated as the most important element of society.

Chapter Five

"They Changed.
They *Really* Changed!"

Inspiring Educators

U P T O T H I S P O I N T, this book has been focused on the adolescents in the comic book club at MLKHS. But of course, some key adults were involved. The Opening Doors and Building Bridges program at MLKHS relies on a small staff of dedicated young adults and parent volunteers who work extremely hard for the teens involved in the after-school initiative.

Regarding the comic book club, three adults in particular impacted the group. These educators are Phil DeJean, the club instructor; Rebecca Fabiano, the program director; and Patricia Ayala, a graduate student at Teachers College, Columbia University, and an assistant to the club. Beyond their staggering amount of other duties, each of these three people played an important role in furthering the club as a whole and helping individual students. This help went beyond designing and publishing comic books. These adults led MLKHS students through unenviable situations ranging from homelessness to abusive relationships to school suspensions. They acted as mediators between the students and their guardians, teachers, school administrators, and social workers. They advised the students on important life decisions when no other adults were available or interested. In that effort, Phil, Rebecca, and Patricia sacrificed their own time, and in some cases, their personal relationships and their careers, to make sure that a student made the train, passed his algebra test, or had a blanket for a cold night. Without these people, the club would not exist—but to be frank, some of the students might not exist either.

"Ms. Fab"

Rebecca Fabiano founded the Opening Doors and Building Bridges program at MLKHS in 1999 with a grant that she initiated from the Lincoln Square Business Improvement District. When the proposal was accepted, Rebecca deferred plans for joining the Peace Corps to take helm at Opening Doors. Over the seven years that she directed the program, she guided it from a small cadre of seventy-five participants to a schoolwide association that has impacted thousands of teenagers. Her goals for the program were ambitious. She aimed to establish a bastion of social and academic support—a place where students could go after school to become better learners and better people. She quickly launched an investment club, poetry forum, and student-teacher basketball tournament. She also looked for opportunities to help the students take trips out of the city and experience other places, leading to what I imagine must be the first and only snowboarding club at a New York City afterschool program. But she also wanted the MLKHS students to forge a better relationship with the surrounding Lincoln Center community, which has had a negative perception of the school since it opened in 1975. One observer of MLKHS stated flatly, "The place seems jinxed."[1] To help bring the students and the community closer together, Rebecca established for the teenagers a community scavenger hunt, a "magical mystery tour" of the neighborhood, and local paid internships.

Rebecca's role as a youth developer is best exemplified by her formation of the school rock band at MLKHS. A student approached her with the idea, which other program directors might have unequivocally rejected. Yet rather than citing the program's lack of financial resources, musical equipment, club advisers, permission from the principal, or space in the school for a very loud band, Rebecca told this student what she promised all of the program participants—that she would do everything in her power to try. The effort had to be mutual, however; students were equally responsible for the success or failure of everything at the Opening Doors program. Hence, Rebecca asked this particular student to submit a request to her in writing for the school rock band.

The proposal required an account of the band's goals, list of participants, practice schedule, musical styles, and potential songs. Rebecca insisted on this proposal because she knew it would (a) measure the student's commitment to establishing a school band, (b) introduce the student to the important business skill of proposal preparation, and (c) hone the student's basic writing skills through a personally relevant assignment. Some days later the student returned to her with a proposal in hand. True to her word, Rebecca scrounged up some money, secured beat-up instruments, found a club adviser, obtained permission from the skeptical principal, and located a space for the band to rehearse—the school's garage. The MLKHS rock band was born.

Rebecca's commitment to the comic book club was just as fervent. When we first met at the school in 2004, she shook my hand then said, "When do we start?" There was no question in her mind that a comic book club would form at MLKHS. She had a room scheduled, supplies set aside, and a list of students ready to participate. Together we mapped a plan for launching the club, including the schedule, time line, necessary materials, and—of prime importance—the instructor, Phil DeJean. Rebecca's enthusiasm for the club was contagious. Phil was eager to get under way, and afterschool participants were anxious to learn about how they could get involved. Rebecca helped to design the recruiting flyer, which she posted around the cafeteria and in the hallways. As she taped each flyer to the wall, she smoothed it out with her hand and said, "This is going to work."

Once the comic book club got under way, Rebecca visited frequently to ensure that things proceeded smoothly. When she learned that the group needed special markers, she ordered them. When she saw that the club members' sketches on loose sheets of typing paper were falling on the floor all around them, she supplied sketchbooks. The club members were interested in learning more about the history of comics; Rebecca arranged a field trip to the Museum of Comics and Cartoon Art in downtown Manhattan and covered their admission fee. The participants were well aware of Rebecca's dedication to their success, and they frequently demonstrated appreciation by sharing their comic books with her. "Check it out, Ms. Fab," they said as they flipped through the pages of their works in progress. Rebecca always responded with praise, but she also asked questions and encouraged the club members to talk about their work: "Tell me about this." "What is your inspiration for this character?" "How do you achieve this effect?" "What does this story say about you?" And Rebecca asked follow-up questions. If their responses were insufficient ("I dunno" or

"I guess"), she chided them: "Is that how you'll respond when you're a famous comic book designer being interviewed by *Rolling Stone*?" The quality responses then began to flow.

About midway through the first year of the club, Rebecca recognized how much progress the MLKHS comic book club was making, and she began to promote its success to others in the afterschool community. She arranged for program managers from TASC to visit the club in action. Before these site visits, Rebecca informed the club members that adults would be paying a visit and that the students should prepare brief statements about their comics and the process of creating them. The visitors were consistently impressed with the quality of the reading, writing, listening, and speaking skills that the club seemed to nurture. They were equally awed by the extent of research that informed the comic books and the students' wide-ranging knowledge of social and cultural trends in the United States and Japan. Practitioners in nonprofit youth development should note that these arranged visits, and the students' abilities to communicate about their work, served not merely to inform people in the field about "best practices." Later in the year, Rebecca requested funding from TASC in order to print the student publication. They granted nearly $1,000.

In the second year of the club, Rebecca forged a strong relationship with Jennifer Stark, the community relations manager at the nearby Barnes & Noble. Jennifer agreed to host an event at the store for the MLKHS comic book club, which I envisioned as a simple exhibit of the student comic books. Rebecca had another plan. She intended to institute a panel discussion that recognized the students as experts who would share their knowledge and experiences with others. Her goal was to present not just the remarkable art and writing that the teens had produced but also the youths themselves as models of proud, accomplished community members. The students were to dress nicely, sit at a large table on a raised platform, speak into microphones, use fancy pens to write on fresh notepads, drink from crystal glasses of water, shake hands with funders and community leaders, and field questions from attendees.

Over one hundred people attended, including family members, other students, and educators from across the city. A group of third-graders from the comic book club at nearby PS 51 sat on the floor right in front of the podium, their eyes wide. Rebecca introduced the club members as some of the most skilled and talented comic book makers in the city, and she encouraged the audience to draw on them as a resource for learning about manga and comics. The students described their respective comics to an attentive crowd and then answered questions from the audience about their ideas, personalities, advice for young artists, plans for the future, and ideas for new comics. Before signing autographs, the students answered each of the questions with clear voices and bright smiles—exactly as Rebecca, standing on the side of the room, had prepared them to do.

Along with promoting and advancing the comic book club as a group, Rebecca had a sense for what individual students needed to succeed in school and in life. I often found her away from her desk in consultation with a student struggling with a geometry formula or in dire need of personal advice. In the comic book club, she perceived that two of the members in particular would benefit from knowing firsthand that their skills in comic book design could translate into gainful employment. She consulted with me about the idea of internships for the Comic Book Project, which resulted in two in-house paid positions. Erick (featured in chapter 8) became the "scan master"— he scanned into Photoshop over one thousand comic books created by elementary school students in Cleveland. He rotated the images, adjusted the brightness and contrast settings, cropped a selection from each scan, and posted the comics in the Cleveland website gallery for that year.[2] Kischer (featured in chapter 13), the most skilled artist to come through the club, became a cover designer for the national launch of CBP in the 2005–06 school year. Figure 5.1 is the cover that she designed for the publication that featured work from students in cities across the United States. Rebecca insisted that both Erick and Kischer be paid by check. She helped them to open bank accounts, fill out deposit slips, and manage their funds.

Needless to say, Rebecca worked extremely hard as the director of Opening Doors, but exhaustion was not the only reason for her decision to resign at the close of the 2006 season. She became frustrated at missed opportunities for growth and improvement of the program. She believed that she had accomplished everything possible within the confines of the funding and resources that were provided to the program, along with the extensive support that she was able to conjure on her own. Moreover, the devolution of MLKHS from one school to two, then four, then six was a disaster from her perspective. As schools competed for resources and space in the building, it became ever more difficult to run a successful and efficient afterschool program. With each new school came a new set of policies, new staff, new students. Furthermore, each additional school brought in its own community partners, as mandated by the New York City Department of Education's small schools initiative. Unfortunately, these nonprofit

FIGURE 5.1 COVER DESIGN BY KISCHER

organizations did not work well together, opting instead to compete for students and funds. Rebecca saw all of this happen at the expense of the students themselves; the situation took a toll on their academic performance, social development, and mental health. She made the extremely difficult decision to leave the program that she had started from scratch. Always looking to maximize the success of Opening Doors, Rebecca spearheaded the hiring of her own replacement, Shonda Streete.

Of all the initiatives and clubs that Rebecca instituted at MLKHS, she was particularly proud of the comic book club. The young participants inspired and humbled her with their dedication and development as artists, writers, and community members. She witnessed the club members morph from shy doodlers in a corner of the cafeteria to a well-respected group of communicators. They found voices for themselves in the processes of reading and writing, and Rebecca felt honored to have helped facilitate their personal transformations. She was also proud of herself for utilizing the comic book club as a vehicle to help the teens navigate "systems" ranging from social to educational to monetary. Their maturation became most evident to her on those early mornings when she accompanied scholarship students on their way to the Center for Cartoon Studies to Penn Station. As the train pulled away, Rebecca realized that she had had a hand in turning some troubled children into responsible young adults. She told me, "They changed. They *really* changed!"

Patricia

Patricia Ayala came to Teachers College in New York City from Mexico on a Fulbright Fellowship in 2001. She began her master's of education degree in art education by exploring the intersections of art, society, health, and schooling in multicultural settings. It was not until she came to the United States that she began to investigate the native arts of Mexico; she became fascinated by the ancient line drawings of the Aztecs and realized that there was not a thorough explanation of this art for children. After putting her young daughter to bed, writing papers for graduate courses, and researching her thesis, Patricia wrote through the nights, and subsequently published, the children's book *Marcos Movement: El Movimiento de Marcos* in 2003, dedicating it to "all the children of the world who have not yet breathed the air of freedom and justice."[3] In this bilingual book, Patricia recreated drawings from ancient Mexican manuscripts to tell the tale of Marcos, a masked young boy who changed the world for the better by listening to and learning from others.

Patricia joined the Comic Book Project in 2004 as a graduate assistant. Previously she had designed her own comics as a way of communicating with youths, and she was well versed in the rich history of comics in Mexico.[4] As the project was expanding nationally, Patricia assumed the responsibility of managing the dozens of sites in New York City. She also started to assist the club at MLKHS on Thursday afternoons. Patricia performed the necessary tasks that moved the club forward—taking attendance, distributing supplies, scanning artwork, escorting students to the cafeteria. As the students became familiar with Patricia, however, they began to rely on her for more than organizational support. At first they wanted to know about her travels to and from Mexico. Her weeks-long delay at the border after a visit home became an exaggerated legend among the teenagers. Soon thereafter the students began to ask Patricia for advice about their comics. They invited her to review their work for language and consistency. They sought her opinion on their characters, whether she found them unique and engaging. Patricia always provided praise accompanied by practical recommendations for improvement.

In time, the club members sought Patricia's advice on more than comics. She became a sounding board for the students' concerns about life, including deteriorating situations at home, ongoing feuds with teachers, and sensitive discussions about opposite-sex relationships. After Rebecca left the Opening Doors program, it was Patricia who became a surrogate parent for many of the comic book club members. When a club member was having trouble obtaining a guardian's signature on a permission slip or scholarship form, Patricia took the long subway ride to the student's home in Brooklyn or the Bronx; she did not return to Manhattan until she obtained what the student needed. Just as Rebecca had done in previous years, Patricia accompanied students to Penn Station to see them on their way to the comics workshop in Vermont. Sensing the students' needs to experience more than the limited scope of school and home, Patricia launched an "explorers" club at MLKHS. Every Saturday she accompanied a group of students around New York City to museums, comics shops, university campuses, the Cloisters, even the annual Mermaid Parade at Coney Island. Through Patricia's guidance, the students discovered some of the reasons why New York City was such a popular destination for everyone else in the world.

Patricia was not the only person in her family to be profoundly affected by experiences at MLKHS. Every Thursday Patricia's daughter accompanied her to the club. At first, eleven-year-old Alessandra sat in a corner doing homework or reading, but the MLKHS students quickly elevated her excitement about manga. Soon she became just as rabid a fan of *Naruto*, *Bleach*, and all the other manga that the teenagers were reading. They inspired their new young protégé to draw and write stories and eventually create her own original manga, and agreed to include Alessandra's comics in the culminating publications. As manga became a bond between Alessandra and the high school students at MLKHS, the Japanese comics also forged a connection between Alessandra and her mother. Living on their own in New York City, Patricia and Alessandra shared manga as a scholarly interest and creative pursuit. Patricia saw manga become a mainstay in her daughter's reading regimen; Alessandra witnessed manga become a core of her mother's career. The daughter also gained a new perspective of her mother's dedication to young people in need. That is a lesson she will not soon forget.

"Mr. D"

Rebecca, Patricia, and the other adults at the Opening Doors program at MLKHS were integral to the success of the comic book club, but the adult who played the most crucial role was Phil DeJean, the club instructor. Phil, an art teacher at one of the schools in the building, had been filling in as the afterschool chess instructor when he overheard some of the program staff discussing the possibilities of a comic book club. Rebecca approached Phil with the idea of becoming the club instructor, and he relished the opportunity. As it turns out, he had been planning a comic book club himself, and the Opening Doors initiative provided the structure and support to get it under way. My first meeting with Phil introduced me to the glow of energy and exuberance that surrounded him. He abounded with enthusiasm for what he believed could be accomplished in a comic book club at MLKHS. He spoke in a jackhammer of sentences about his influences, goals, methods, interests—leaving me momentarily thunderstruck. In response to my silence, he snapped his fingers and quoted a dancehall reggae song by Smiley Culture: "My kids love it, and so does my mother." I had no idea what he was talking about, but I immediately warmed to his unique style and personality.

Phil was no stranger to comic books. He began to collect and then create comic books as a young child. He started his own series, called "Korny Stuph"; it emulated the comics in his personal collection—*Sandman*, *House of Mystery*, *Ghost Rider*, and dozens more. In a short time, Korny Stuph featured over one hundred issues in various sizes and designs. A middle school teacher recognized Phil's passion for art and the abilities that he had developed through his comics, and she encouraged him to take the entry exam for LaGuardia High School of Music & Art and Performing Arts. He was accepted, and his educational outlook drastically shifted from an outcast among restless youths in the Bronx to a budding artist with compatible peers and friends. Phil recalled his high school years at LaGuardia as some of the best in his life. It was a place where teachers cultivated a community of learning in and through the arts and where students shared ideas, goals, and successes. The one downside to LaGuardia, however, was leaving the school. Students from MLKHS frequently crossed the street to pick fights with the young artists, musicians, and dancers as they exited LaGuardia. As a high school student, Phil was nervous about stepping into MLKHS's menacing shadow, unaware that one day he would step through the metal detector to teach there.

When that time came in 2003, Phil's worst nightmares of MLKHS came true. He distributed paper and pencils for his art students to provide a sample of their drawing skills on the first day of class. One student shouted, "We can't draw!" Suddenly, the pencils, paper, and everything else on the desks were sailing through the air—chaos. From then on, Phil struggled to connect with the students in his art classes. Some could draw but had no direction, others had lost interest in art after being told for years that they lacked talent, and others tuned out entirely with their heads on the table or eyes on the ceiling.

After school, however, was a different story. The announcement of the comic book club quickly lured a small group of dedicated enthusiasts into the art room. Phil described the students' initial attempts as "hacking away" at Pokemon and Dragon Ball Z characters. He asked them to put down their pencils and simply talk a bit about themselves, something that they had rarely done in school. He wanted to know about *their* ideas and what kinds of stories they would want to tell if given the chance. The stories emerged: love relationships, escaping the school and the city, fighting at home. The students began to communicate with each other, and they soon discovered three things. First, they shared similar life experiences and found in each other sympathetic ears. Second, they held a mutual respect for comics, specifically manga. Finally, they gathered that Phil would do anything he possibly could to help them be successful.

Because the club attracted members of different skill levels and experiences, Phil established a process that allowed everyone to work at their own pace. At the beginning of a club session, he introduced a topic, sometimes a general art technique like shading or perspective and other times more specific instructions related to the design of fingers or eyelids. Each presentation lasted no longer than five minutes. Rather than practicing that particular technique as they might in an art class, the students dove into their comics or drafted ideas in their sketchbooks. Phil reminded them of the technique as the need arose, and they incorporated those skills over time rather than as a supervised practice session. In this manner, the students focused on the stories and characters of their own creation, but they also learned practical art techniques along the way. Phil guided writing in the comics in a similar manner. Some students had notebooks full of written stories, and others struggled mightily with a few words. He encouraged all of them, giving some students inspiration for reducing their long stories to essential captions or dialogue and other students the encouragement to write freely without the fear of a grade or red-ink corrections—spelling, grammar, and punctuation could be fixed later.

As the comics were developed in the club, Phil honed specific skills in students who showed an interest or ability in certain areas. A student who seemed to enjoy inking received from Phil a special set of pens and a discourse on the techniques of cross-hatching. Students who were stuck in their stories or frustrated by undeveloped drawing abilities found themselves on the computer learning how to use Photoshop. For those students who loved manga but had little or no experience in making art, Phil often reminded: "I don't care if you draw stick figures as long as they improve every week." On the other end of the spectrum, for those students who had extremely well-developed art skills, Phil was not afraid to give them criticism and ideas for improving even more. Those capable artists appreciated Phil's feedback—they wanted their manga to be as good as possible. Without the resources that more privileged young artists might have received, such as private art lessons or precollege classes, Phil was their only conduit to artistic improvement. Some of these students had applied to LaGuardia but were rejected because of poor grades or, in more than one case, incomplete submissions of drawings on typing paper. Phil advised them on how to build a professional portfolio and present it with confidence.

Phil regularly reminded the students that the skills developed in the comic book club could be parlayed into a career. "Name the last movie you saw," he told the students. "Was it based on a comic book?" More often than not, the answer was yes. Phil instilled in the teens a belief that their work was just as important as that of any other comic book creator. He told them to expect that their stories and concepts would improve over time, but it was important for them to share their comics with as wide an audience as possible while they were young. He believed that the publications, exhibits, panel discussions, and other club activities in which the students participated were excellent opportunities for exposure and networking. Phil's greatest fear was that the students would replicate the life of Henry Darger, an unassuming man who worked as a janitor in Chicago. It was only after Darger died in 1973 that his landlord discovered the enormous collection of art and writing that Darger had created over the course of his life. Darger became recognized as one of the most innovative artists of the twentieth century; his works are featured in prestigious museums and galleries. Darger never knew any of the notoriety because he kept his work to himself. Phil dreaded a similar situation for students at MLKHS, who were often self-conscious about the quality of their work and nervous about sharing it with others outside the club.

The personal connections that Phil forged with the comic book club members were unprecedented. The students came to know him as an ally, a person whom they could trust with personal issues or sensitive information. Part of this trust was based on his acceptance of the students for who they were, perhaps because of his comparable experiences growing up in the Bronx. Yet another aspect of the relationship between Phil and the students was his own knowledge of and infatuation with comics and manga, which matched the students'. Phil was able to converse with the comic book club members about the very thing that made them feel strange and excluded at MLKHS. He was just as keen as they were to keep abreast of new publications, artists, and trends in manga around the world. Phil saw in manga exactly what the students did—multidimensional characters with complex lives that did not exist merely because a marketing team or television network brought them to life. Together, Phil and the club members found meaning and depth in manga characters and stories. Through this art and literature, they formed a resilient bond.

Phil himself went through a personal transformation because of the comic book club. He became inspired by the students' commitment to their comics, which encouraged him to work even harder as the mentor of the group. He stayed late after school not just when the club met on Thursdays but other days as well, especially if students needed personal attention in their comic book designs and layouts. In part to give the students extra time to work on their comic books, he led an anime club on Tuesday afternoons. Some students watched anime movies and shows on DVD in front of the class while others scratched away at their comics in the back. Toward the end of each school year, Phil worked feverishly on the publications. He coordinated students to create the covers, secured copy from the Opening Doors staff for the front matter, scanned all of the student work, notated the layout of pages, wrote instructions for the print house, and prepared the final files on CD and in print. Through these long days and late nights, Phil often said aloud, "It's all about the kids." The fact that he had helped to build a community of engaged artists and learners motivated him to put in the extra (unpaid) effort. Phil told me he felt as though he had created his own little LaGuardia.

In contrast with the strong rapport that Phil had built with the members of the comic book club and the boon that the club had been for the Opening Doors program, his relationship with his school and its principal soured. In the spring of 2008, the school ousted Phil from his teaching position, placing him in a reassignment center known among New York City teachers as the "rubber room."

The students in the club were crushed. When the announcement came through that Phil could no longer lead the club, tears and angry curses erupted in the club-room. Patricia tried to calm the students, but there was little she could say. She did not know when or if Phil would return to the club. It was unlikely that his case would be resolved so late in the school year. The enormity of the situation settled in as students held each other, stormed out of the building, demanded answers. But in the end, all they were left with was a piercing sense of loss and injustice that ran deep. Especially for the longtime members of the group, the person who had convinced them that they could achieve great things in school and in the world was now gone. Their unfinished comics on the table were fitting metaphors for how the year would end and how the club would be affected.

However, as a tribute to Phil and out of respect for their own substantial efforts over the course of the year, one thing that the club members did resolve was that the publication would get finished. Patricia arranged for them to come to the computer lab at Teachers College to scan their work and add the finishing touches in Photoshop. Phil, in an unofficial role, gathered the contents of the book and pulled it together for printing. As usual, he worked tirelessly on it. Although it missed the target date in

June, the book was printed over the summer of 2008. The students returned to Teachers College on a hot July day, and the books were distributed. As before, the club members first read through them in silence, then guffawed over stories and characters in their friends' comics. Unlike past distribution days, however, this one was rather somber. It was unclear whether these young comic book designers would ever again meet as a group. If the comic book club were to continue, they had doubts about whether it would have the same meaning. Without Mr. DeJean, comics seemed to hold just a bit less power.

Part II

The Students

Chapter Six

Stardaisha

STARDAISHA WAS ONE OF THE ORIGINAL MEMBERS of the comic book club at MLKHS. She was one of the first to see the flyer, one of the first to sign up for the club, and always first with her pencils sharpened and ready to create manga. She rushed in every Thursday afternoon with a knapsack stuffed with manga books, loose sheets of her own sketches, a variety of drawing utensils and erasers, and a number of decaying sketchbooks. To anyone else, the sketchbooks seemed a random collection of pencil-drawn manga characters and story snippets in various stages of development. Stardaisha, however, knew the contents of every page of every book. Pages 1 through 8 of sketchbook #1 plotted the travails of Casandra, a fox-demon-girl. Casandra lived in shame of her foxtail and pointed ears and wished more than anything to be human. Pages 9 through 14 were filled with drawings of Casandra's cat, Pebbles, cute and gray with large, pleading eyes. Her drawings placed the cat at different angles and perspectives, a comprehensive self-guided study in figure anatomy.

These pages and the dozens more that comprised Stardaisha's collection accounted for the work that she had composed on her own time. She used the preliminary sketches and story suggestions from her sketchbooks to draft manga under the tutelage of Phil DeJean during the club hours. For the most part, Phil left Stardaisha to her own devices; he made brief suggestions about the appearance of a finger here or a cloud there. He realized Stardaisha's primary need: the unfettered space to explore her own creative ideas. At the start of every Thursday session, Stardaisha said aloud,

"Here we go again." She did not utter these words out of boredom or with a roll of her eyes. She said them as though a runner on the starting blocks before a race—pencil in her hand and ready to disappear into her manga world of fantasy. Before she began to draw and write, however, Stardaisha stared at the wall for half a minute or so, her eyes unfocused. As she explained it, she formed in her mind the concept of her story by imagining how the characters would develop over the course of the next few panels of her comic. Just before getting to work, Stardaisha nodded her head with the confidence of knowing what she would accomplish in the next ninety minutes. After school, Stardaisha was in control.

In school, however, Stardaisha was caught in the middle of MLKHS's transition from a large high school to six smaller entities. Her schedule was jumbled, so that she would be assigned to several sections of the same course. Attempts to resolve these problems resulted in an administrative quagmire. Lost in the shuffle, Stardaisha began to struggle. She experienced a lack of support through these years from school administrators, who seemed anxious to push out MLKHS's final graduating class in 2005 and get on with the small-school plan. As a result, Stardaisha shut down. She moped through the halls and sat quietly in the back of her classes. Her class notes, homework, and returned tests were riddled with manga faces donning a variety of sneering expressions. The girl who had previously exhibited a passion for learning now viewed school as an adversary. Once the last bell rang, however, Stardaisha was able to concentrate on manga, and she snapped back to her former boisterous self. All of her pent-up energy came forth during the comic book club, where she rowdily joked with friends before engulfing herself in the next installment of Casandra and Pebbles.

Hidden among the crowd during the school day, Stardaisha became a leader after school. Her work ethic in creating manga was a model for other students; they discerned from her actions the extent of time and energy necessary in order to become a successful high school *mangaka* and gain a coveted spot in the culminating publication. When participants became unfocused during the club session, Phil simply nodded his head toward Stardaisha, hard at work and fully absorbed in her art and writing. The others quickly got the message and buckled down. Stardaisha mentored new club members by establishing a process of drafting and outlining, which led to more fully developed comics later in the school year. She had learned through personal experience the disastrous outcomes of rushing into a completed manga without first sketching and planning. The characters became undefined and the story muddled if proper steps were not taken to map the direction of the comic book. Stardaisha was ready to share examples of her own manga that had gone awry with novices so that they could learn from her mistakes. Stardaisha's commitment to helping others in the group was instrumental in cultivating a community of young comic book makers at MLKHS.

Among the club members, Stardaisha was a pioneer in the use of Photoshop to color her artwork and design the text in her comic book. She sensed that black-and-white line drawings did not serve her dynamic characters and their range of emotions well. A more colorful approach would highlight the humor of the story and help to convey the fast-paced action sequences that infused her manga. Colored pencils, crayons, or markers were out of the question. Using such tools would consume too much time late in the year and force her to either reduce the length of her comic book or rush through the coloring process. At Phil's suggestion, Stardaisha opened the decrepit flatbed scanner and powered up the old computer to scan her pages into Photoshop. Phil showed Stardaisha how to use the "magic wand" tool to select a desired area of an image and fill it with color. From there on, Stardaisha began to color her comic, first importing the color for the skin of each character, then clothes, followed by hues for the backgrounds and other secondary images. Through this technological application, Stardaisha added an entirely new element to her manga and learned a valuable skill along the way.

These early phases of the comic book club were Stardaisha's opportunity to hone a process and demonstrate a product that would influence many students at MLKHS and others outside the school as well. Manga fans from Chicago, Los Angeles, and Cleveland connected with Casandra and Pebbles as characters, and therefore with Stardaisha as an artist and storyteller. These people far from New York City sought to know about her ideas and plans for future manga. The club established Stardaisha as an up-and-coming force in manga, a person who mattered in the world, if not at her school. In order to remain a club participant, however, Stardaisha had to fulfill her academic obligations. Her case is one in which the club did not necessarily improve academic performance; it did, however, keep her inside school walls and involved enough in her academic courses to obtain a diploma. Along with her comic book work, Stardaisha's graduation proved to be an inspiration for other students. She navigated her way through turbulent times at MLKHS by relying on her comics as a bridge to the classes, tests, and credits that the school required of her. Her focus on comics as a life raft in a sea of school turmoil became a model for others to get through MLKHS in one piece.

Gallery Notes

Stardaisha's main character Casandra was born half fox and half human, but "she thinks her life would be happier if she was all human." Casandra longs to fit in. She would readily swap her special characteristics for acceptance by humans. The parallels to Stardaisha are substantial. The real high schooler wandered the halls of MLKHS feeling like an outcast. Her desire and ability to create manga set her apart from peers outside of the comic book club. Both Stardaisha and her creation Casandra found themselves simultaneously blessed and cursed with unique traits: Casandra, the ability to communicate with animals and produce sharp claws; Stardaisha, the knack for developing and designing cute and humorous Japanese manga characters. Although Casandra does not look like a teenage African American girl in New York City, Stardaisha created the character as a manga likeness of herself—conflicted about her role in school and society and anxious about how she might use her special artistic aptitude in "real life." Like Casandra, Stardaisha had few people in her life to approach for advice. She was often left to brood alone about her predicament, burying herself in panel after panel of original manga.

Casandra perks up with the discovery of Pebbles, a distressed little cat. Their compatibility and future companionship is best represented by the similar design of their eyes—inquisitive, round saucers. Casandra readily adopts Pebbles. The fox-girl names the cat and buys Pebbles a fine bowl of beef stew. When Pebbles wants more than her share, Casandra playfully chides the cat. Clearly, Pebbles has found a caring, loving keeper on the lookout for the cat's best interests and well-being. Stardaisha longed for the same at MLKHS—someone who could guide her through the confusing maze of hallways, the regularly shifting schedules, the rush of faces and names that shifted from one school to another. Phil DeJean guided Stardaisha in creating comics, but she longed for a more comprehensive learning environment where her skills could be considered an asset rather than a distraction. Pebbles rustled in the underbrush and was discovered by a savior—Casandra. In contrast, Stardaisha was lucky enough to discover for herself the comic book club, but it was a short respite in the long sleepwalk that school came to be for her.

Casandra and Pebbles turn out to be a formidable team. When a giant rattlesnake appears and terrorizes the townspeople, Casandra summons forth from her wrist the "demon sword." We now know something about the reason behind the description of Casandra as part demon in the first panel of the comic book. Before she jumps into battle, however, Casandra ensures the safety of Pebbles, telling the cat to run and hide. But Pebbles, too, has transformed with the arrival of the monster reptile. The once shy, mewing kitty is now larger than Casandra and sports ominous black eyes, daggered fangs, and white-hot flames emanating from her tail and paws. Now bonded as a fighting force, Casandra and Pebbles square up to face the danger before them. Interestingly, Stardaisha never shows graphic violence in her comic book, unlike most of the boys and some of the girls in the club. She chooses instead to focus on the character and story development. "We have enough violence around us," she once remarked. There was another reason for refraining from violence in the comic book, however. Stardaisha wanted her comic book to reach as wide an audience as possible, including young children.

Stardaisha's combination of written text and visual imagery is a prime example of how the medium of comic books can help youths think critically about the depth of language. The second panel of her comic book features a wealth of "word art" that speaks to the range of our semiotic systems and how pliable they can be in the hands of a creative thinker like Stardaisha. The heroine Casandra hears an unusual sound in the nearby bushes—we understand the nature of the sound via the word "rustle," but we also feel and hear the sound through the appearance of the word: the broken font and increasing size of the capital letters. Casandra's alarm at this sound is made evident by the size and boldness of the letters in "Who's There?" especially when compared with the demure letters of the caption in the first panel or Casandra's cooing to the cat in the third panel.

Most interesting, though, is the giant exclamation point above Casandra's head. This use of demonstrative punctuation as a conveyance of emotion is common in manga and a practice regularly adopted by Stardaisha and others in the comic book club. The variety of punctuation marks, fonts, letter sizes, and colors of words indicates the importance of text in Stardaisha's comic book and her attention to the details of language. In short, writing is one of Stardaisha's tools for communication. Her words, along with her art, set an early standard for how manga could become a forum for expression at MLKHS.

Chapter Seven

C-Wiz

IF THE PERVASIVE IMAGE OF A TEENAGER is that of a raucous, unruly, undisciplined adolescent, C-Wiz splintered the typecast with his gentle, mature demeanor. He always chose his spoken words carefully, practically closing his eyes in contemplation of how to phrase his statements. Listeners found themselves paying heed to his words, which were few but eloquent and noteworthy. Manner of speech was merely a sample of the mystique that the teen generated around his own persona. His preferred name, C-Wiz, went unexplained. Everyone in the club, including Phil, referred to him by this moniker without issue. Of even greater mystery was C-Wiz's process in creating manga. He often drifted in and out of the club, sometimes disappearing for weeks at a stint. There were times when peers thought him missing, adding to his air of eccentricity. Yet he always returned with impressive finished work in hand, as though he had been sitting at his spot in the clubroom all along, a specter of comic booking. C-Wiz's commitment to creating manga convinced Phil and the staff at Opening Doors to overlook his sketchy attendance record at the club. It was clear to the adults and youths in the program that C-Wiz's creative process was mostly a solitary one and something that should go undisrupted.

C-Wiz was a spiritual young man. At exhibits and panel discussions featuring the club, he told audiences that be believed men should look inside themselves to find their inner women and women should find their inner men. The result, according to C-Wiz, would be world peace and understanding. He stated on several occasions that art was the answer to end wars for all time. He postulated that people who shared art had better understandings of each other because they were compelled to consider how, why, when, and where the art was created, leading to an appreciation for diverse peoples and cultures. Comic books in particular were effective for fostering peace, in his opinion, because the stories combined with art became powerful tools for the exchange of ideas. Unlike most of the other students in the club, C-Wiz believed that his comics held a greater significance than the characters and their words, exploits, and actions. He created manga as a vehicle for social commentary and a tool for social justice.

Sometimes people outside the club, usually adults, regarded C-Wiz with skepticism. When others responded to C-Wiz's quiet words of spirituality with a strange look or a shrug, he simply smiled with a knowing posture. "Don't get discouraged by people who don't believe in you," C-Wiz said. "They'll come around if you give them some time, and if you give them enough to think about." C-Wiz was extremely confident in himself but never smug. He treated other people with respect and strove to gain knowledge by tapping others for their views of the world. After an exhibit in 2005, C-Wiz asked me about my work; he framed his question in an unusual way: "What is your impact?" He did not inquire what I did for a living or request a label for my vocation. Rather he wanted to know if I was trying to make the world a better place and what he himself might procure from my experience and apply to his own life. I had to think for a few seconds—what was my impact? I responded by saying that I was unsure of my impact, but I was trying to develop opportunities for young people to have an enormous impact in the future. As usual, C-Wiz nearly closed his eyes and took a few seconds to respond: "That works for me, and your impact has been felt." He smiled and shook my hand.

Inquisitive by nature, C-Wiz cherished learning about and experiencing new ideas and concepts. When a school project or assignment offered him the opportunity to advance his knowledge and understanding of the world and its people, he embraced the task wholeheartedly. But if homework or standardized test preparation constrained his creative and exploratory efforts, C-Wiz elected to brush them off as unnecessary. He generally received good grades but was a thorn to some teachers who disapproved of his individualistic outlook. In the comic book club, however, individuality was a welcome quality. C-Wiz was unimpeded in his search for human compassion through comic books, and his unconventional work methods were fostered and honed rather than denigrated as slothful or inconsistent. As an artist and writer, C-Wiz advanced his narrative skills through the comic book club. More importantly, though, the club established for C-Wiz as a person an outlet for his convictions and passions about human nature and its ability to overcome dark times and base actions. I came to see C-Wiz as a truth-seeker, a modern philosopher; the comic book club was his academy and his comic books the tomes that illuminated his ideas.

Gallery Notes

C-Wiz's two-page story, titled "Choso's Point of View," is a contemplative, sorrowful introspection by a female character from the planet Ra-Xephon, a name derived from the anime science fiction series *RahXephon*.[1] The story begins with Choso crying over a bowl of food and chopsticks on her lap, ruminating about the human love of her life, now absent. The third panel of the comic book features a harrowing image of leaning steel girders and severed cables, as Choso narrates: "With the Towers of Ra-Xephon gone, I began to wonder was it all worth it?" If this image does not bring to mind parallel events on earth, C-Wiz makes the point explicit with a depiction of the burning World Trade Center. He contrasts the enormity of the destruction with a single red pendant placed on a simple white table, presumably a gift to Choso from her human lover. C-Wiz reiterates the contrast with a mushroom cloud and the same pendant dangling from Choso's finger. Choso says, "It's 'human nature' for them to destroy one another!" She is trying to be flippant about the loss of the man, but the ache in her heart matches the size of the gaping hole in the earth at Ground Zero in downtown Manhattan.

Stepping back from the comic book, it is important to remember that C-Wiz and the other members of the comic book club were between the ages of seven and fifteen in 2001 when terrorists hijacked airplanes and slammed them into the World Trade Center. The students were likely in school that Tuesday morning. If they did not witness in person the destruction, fire, smoke, and billow of ash, they certainly experienced the unnerving aftermath that all New Yorkers faced: loss of loved ones, friends, or neighbors; concerns about security; stoppage of services; questions about the future of the city. Of course, they also were subject to the constantly repeating images that everyone in the world faced, inescapable for anyone with a television or computer. That day and the images it shaped will remain a part of the lives of all children in New York City, including those who eventually joined the comic book club at MLKHS. Art became a way for many young people in the city to try to make sense of the terrorist attacks. The tall sculptures of ABC blocks created by the Youngest Witnesses, compiled by a teacher of prekindergarten students who witnessed the horror up close, is a genuine, if not heart-wrenching, example of the healing power of art.[2]

The comic book club at MLKHS provided teens, several years later, with an outlet to at least attempt to synthesize 9/11 by incorporating the day and its consequences into comic book stories. C-Wiz was able to reconstruct and deconstruct the image of the Twin Towers on 9/11, and thereby convey his lingering distress through the words and emotions of the character Choso. Of course, this image of the burning buildings did not suddenly appear in C-Wiz's comic book. He thought carefully about the lines and shapes as they formed on his paper. He pictured in his mind, then subsequently on the page, the surrounding smaller buildings, the entire financial district, and undoubtedly the people on the streets below. He reminded himself of how the smoke ballooned upward from the fires in the smashed windows, the point of impact on one building higher than the other. Most striking, C-Wiz recalled how sunny and mild the weather was in New York City that day. He purposefully chose a fitting background in Photoshop to insert behind the foreground of his drawings. Through all of these details, C-Wiz exposed underlying meaning in the event by means of his art and writing: the personal cost to Choso, her conflicted thoughts about the event and the humans who caused it, the effect on the earth and her universe. The contrast between the blue sky and destroyed buildings in the middle of the first page is almost as potent as the one in the preceding panel—earth whirling through endless space, a rock among countless other rocks. Choso says: "It's just Earth! Nothing worth saving . . ." C-Wiz may have held the same sentiment.

There is another level on which C-Wiz's story reflects 9/11, and this relationship solidifies the importance of manga in the life of C-Wiz and the other MLKHS club members. C-Wiz referenced *RahXephon*, the popular anime series, manga, and movie about a teenage student and artist named Ayato Kamina. In the story, Tokyo is attacked by an alien force called the Mulians, or Mu. Through mystical forces, music, and philosophy, the citizens of Tokyo and the Mu battle for control of the minds and souls of humankind. The main character Kamina finds that he has the power to control the strange mystical world of RahXephon, and he grapples with his own identity and relationship with humankind throughout the series. The story captivated C-Wiz, who identified with Kamina—both adolescents experienced terrible attacks in their cities, and both had to look within themselves to understand how such a thing could happen. By intertwining his story into that of *RahXephon*, C-Wiz balanced his own life experiences with those of a fictional Japanese character. Whether C-Wiz found tangible answers to life's most difficult questions can only be known to C-Wiz, but his artistic and creative willingness to explore these questions inspired the other teenagers around him.

Along with his openness to confront past experiences, C-Wiz demonstrated his maturity—and followed his own advice to find his "inner woman"—by creating his comic book from the perspective of a female character. His was the only case at MLKHS in which the main character of the comic book was a different gender than the story's author. Adult readers of "Choso's Point of View" had a difficult time believing that the story was written and designed by a male teenager. "The aesthetic is so *female*," exclaimed one graduate student during an exhibit of the comic books at Teachers College. It was not merely Chosos's delicate eyes and stylized hair that elicited this statement; the ability of C-Wiz to capture and convey the feelings of the woman was remarkable. On the second page of the story, the water from the shower falls like Choso's tears as she recalls fond memories of the man: "Now I shower, expecting him to bang on the door, needing to use the toilet. I found it hilarious every time!" C-Wiz perceptively recognized that seemingly meaningless details of a relationship are what we remember most after a loved one suddenly disappears from our lives.

C-Wiz's comic ends with a somber poem by Choso: "My life is forever shattered. / No one will ever brighten my eyes like he did. Nothing is the same without him. / It just isn't!" Clearly, Choso's existence has been altered dramatically by external forces. If the reader was unsure of her commitment to the man at the beginning of the story, there is no vagueness about her grief at the end. However, the comic book does not conclude with Choso's sad face, which appears in the penultimate panel. The final panel returns to the destroyed towers of Ra-Xephon, a close-up of the wrecked columns topped by a shattered orb, akin to Fritz Koenig's "The Sphere," a sculpture that now sits in Battery Park after being recovered from the World Trade Center. C-Wiz leaves us with a reminder of an event that has dramatically impacted his life, a cue for us to remember that life is fragile and our impacts are consequential.

Chapter Eight

Erick

ERICK WAS A PROBLEM FOR THE STAFF at Opening Doors. He hung around the program office after school, causing trouble and picking fights. He did not join any of the clubs but opted instead to disrupt as many groups as possible by calling out to friends during hip-hop dance or making silly faces over the monitors during computer class. Rebecca Fabiano recalled that Erick would knowingly cause trouble, then turn around and look at her with a certain pleading in his eyes. He exhibited neither aggression nor anger. She said, "It was more like a plea for help, like 'Now I got your attention—please help me.'" The one place that Erick seemed at peace was in his school art class, taught by Phil DeJean. Phil and Rebecca both prodded Erick to join the comic book club. He often read comics between outbursts, and the club seemed an ideal way to harness his energy and foster his interests. Erick was hesitant at first about the prospect of making comics, however. It was something he felt he could never accomplish, having never accomplished much of anything in his life. Phil and Rebecca worked hard to convince him otherwise, and Erick eventually showed up to the club. The very fact that he came to the correct room at the designated time seemed like a victory.

Erick commenced by drawing violent, gory scenes. He did not bother to set up his fight sequences within a storyline—say, a hero avenging the death of a family member or a villain wreaking turmoil on a city for past wrongs. Instead, Erick's comics dove straight into bloody battles between unnamed characters. These depictions of carnage did not delineate winners and losers. One character delivered a deadly blow to the next, leading to a spray of blood. In the subsequent panel, that same character received his own deathblow from the previously mauled combatant who certainly should have been dead on the ground. Yet both lived to see another panel, in which one kicked his foot directly through the other's neck. The panels continued in this manner: two immortal fighters with an endless supply of blood and brain matter. The text consisted of sound effects. In many ways, Erick's comics were representative of violent shooter videogames. The panels exhibited a sequence in which one event occurred after another, but those events were virtually indistinguishable amid all the blood and guts. Had Erick placed score boxes and a tally underneath each of the characters, his comic would have read like a storyboard for *Doom* or *Max Payne*. Not surprisingly, Erick was a zealous fan of such videogames.

Despite the unilateral focus of his comics, Erick did show promise in his drawing skills. He had a knack for perspective and a unique approach to character design. His panels, though difficult to stomach, exhibited a variety of techniques that Erick had taught himself through the comics in his collection. Because he routinely focused on the action in these comics, Erick took the stories for granted. From his perspective, the stories served only to bolster the violent combat. He breezed through the captions and dialogue to get to "thwaaat" (a karate chop) and "ugggh" (a punch in the gut), which he believed were the heart of the comics. Phil eventually helped Erick understand how shallow comics would be without quality storylines; he asked Erick to narrate a page from one of his most violent comic book creations. Erick started out strong, "This guy slices this guy. Then this guy kills this guy." As he continued with descriptions of the unending, pointless violence, the decrescendo of Erick's voice was noticeable. Through this exercise, Erick realized that plot trumps action in a comic book. As a result, he had drawn his last act of random violence.

Erick's comics matured, as did the adolescent himself. Whereas Erick once did his best to earn the label of "troublemaker," he became dedicated to the comic book club not only as an artist but as a producer of sorts. He began to manage the process of seeing other students' comics from the drawing board to the lightbox to the scanner. He encouraged peers in their work, providing feedback on their characters and story developments. He cultivated an interest in the process of creating comics from a professional perspective, investigating the specific roles of inkers, editors, and color specialists at large comic book publishing companies. Within the span of a few months,

Phil came to rely on Erick as a responsible person who would keep his word and lend a hand whenever asked. The comic book club eventually granted Erick a purpose beyond making others laugh and gaining attention for inappropriate behavior. It established for him a vision of how he could make the most of his high school years and the transition into adulthood.

Rebecca rewarded Erick for his newly developed trustworthiness and dependability. She established an internship position where Erick was paid to assist the Comic Book Project. Every day for over a month, Erick tackled a pile of comic books from elementary and middle school students in Cleveland. He scanned their work and selected a panel from each comic to appear on the project website. Erick accomplished this task without supervision. He set his own schedule based on the availability of the computer lab. He reported back to Rebecca and me on his progress through frequent e-mail updates. If unsure about which portion to select from a certain comic or the spelling of a student's name, Erick put the work in question aside and marked it with a Post-it Note. On several visits to MLKHS, I found Erick in the computer lab working on his internship assignment. I asked if he needed any help, but he seemed insulted by the question. Erick had a handle on what it would take for him to work through the daunting pile of comics and complete the task on schedule. He received the check for his services proudly. Earlier in the year, Erick might have waved the money in the face of a peer. Now, however, he simply smiled, placed the check in his backpack, and said "Thank you."

In 2005, Erick became the first student to receive a scholarship to the summer workshop at the Center for Cartoon Studies in White River Junction, Vermont. Rebecca chose Erick for this honor because of his transformation over the course of the school year. The award was announced at one of the exhibits at Barnes & Noble, a presentation that left Erick speechless with gratitude. Early in July, Rebecca saw Erick off at Penn Station, where he boarded a train with his ticket, bags, and drawing pens. She had never imagined that this once disorderly youth would become a representative of the best and most accomplished students at the Opening Doors program. She and everyone else at Opening Doors was excited to meet Erick after the trip to hear about his experiences and read the comics that he had created during the workshop. They never got the chance. Erick and his family moved to Florida as soon as he returned from Vermont. He continued to remain in contact with Rebecca by e-mailing her on occasion. His latest communication was sent from Iraq, where Erick is serving in the army. (He enlisted in 2007 for a number of reasons, including the effect of 9/11 on him.) A serviceman for his country now, Erick had one simple request: please send over some comics.

Gallery Notes

Erick's one-page comic layout is a testament to the process that he helped to develop at MLKHS, and to his transformation from outsider to authority. He designed the page with Phil and titled it "This Is How We Do It!" Erick and Phil together summarized the progression of comics development from sketchbook to final publication. Erick introduces himself as the narrator in the first panel, establishing himself as a master. The second panel explains how the process begins with "an idea, story, plot or central character." This is a key statement from Erick, a comic book creator who at first thought not a bit about any of these narrative components. Had he been asked to create this page at the start of his comic book career, he would have initiated the process with a knifing or body slam. There would have been little for him to explain since he had no creative process of which to speak. That changed over the course of the club season, however. With this demonstration page, Erick reveals his understanding of the very core of narrative fiction: ideas, plot, and characters. As Erick highlights, the figurative lightbulb must spark before the drawing can begin.

Next step in the process is a rough sketch. Erick is very clear about what a sketch entails: "It doesn't have to be NEAT!" He had witnessed the problems of perfectionism in the creative process. A few extremely skilled artists in the club failed to grasp the concept of a sketch. Every image they drew was endowed with intricate details, which consumed hour after hour of their time, session after session of club meetings. Some would near the completion of a drafted drawing only to obliterate it with an eraser and begin anew. No matter how many times Erick and other club members tried to explain the purpose of creating a rough copy, these artists were too closely tied to precise visual details to complete a larger picture, let alone a comic book. Erick warns against this pitfall in his presentation piece.

A finished sketch leads to the "good paper," two-ply bristol. Then off to the letterer, generally a freshman member of the club responsible for tracing the penciled words with black pens. It is a tiresome task that often takes prodding from senior club members. Erick inserts some humor into the comic as the overexerted letterer moans under Erick's strict oversight. He yells at the letterer: "Shut up and do it," a phrase commonly heard in the clubroom, though never in a malicious way.

The comics are close to completion now. Erick sarcastically begins his "favorite part" in scanning, a process he came to know quite well. He inserts comic relief, making a point of waiting for the scanner to warm up and reminding readers to save their work before the computer crashes, which was a regular occurrence in the clubroom. The computer and scanner were sources of frustration and laughter for the club participants. The frustration stemmed from malfunctions at the most inopportune times—hours before deadline or during presentations for visitors. The laughter resulted from commiseration at the faulty equipment or the inevitable string of curses from a student whose work was devoured by the notorious hard drive. Erick once framed the situation to me by pointing out the irony in the name of his designated school (High School of Arts and Technology) and the fact that the only computer he ever had the chance to use throughout his high school years, outside of his monthlong internship, was the decrepit machine in the comic book clubroom. He smirked and said sarcastically, "Like it's a privilege to use this thing once a week."

Once the comics are colored in Photoshop, Erick explains that the images are imported into publishing software (usually Adobe InDesign), then delivered to the printer. As Erick says, "After that it's outta our hands!" With a wink and a flash of the CD of finished files, Erick concludes the comic with a "Bling!" indicating his faith in the success of his work. Erick signs off by saying "good luck." He is sincere in his best wishes, hoping that others will discover in comics what he unearthed—a life pursuit. Erick found a connection in these pictures and words with life itself. He reflected: "Comic book making is what you make of it, and so is life."

Chapter Nine

Samantha

NO STUDENT WAS MORE DEDICATED to manga than Samantha. The club at MLKHS was a mere two hours in a life consumed by reading, designing, and blogging about Japanese-style comics. For other students, the club may have been the focal point for manga in their lives, but for Samantha the club was primarily a publishing outlet for her comics and an opportunity to build an audience for her original manga characters and stories. She did not attend the club as regularly as most other students, but, like C-Wiz, her commitment to the craft was unquestionable. Samantha produced volumes of original manga based on characters that she developed at home, in school, on the subway, or wherever else she could find a flat surface to place her sketchbook and uncap a pen. Along with her accomplishments in the design of manga, Samantha was a powerful writer. This combination of drawing facility and literary prowess established Samantha as a role model for beginning club members and veterans of the group alike. If making manga had been a school sport, Samantha would have been on the varsity team. Yet because her skills and interests were confined to the small world of artists and writers of the afterschool program, her gifts went largely unnoticed at school.

Samantha's devotion to manga extended beyond the ink in her sketchbooks and the pages of favorite Tokyopop publications. She attended manga and anime conventions, scraping together money for the entrance fees and whatever comics she could afford to buy from the vendors. Samantha also prepared her own comics to present as *doujinshi* at the conventions. In the summer of 2008, she traveled to Baltimore for the Otakon convention, a three-day event dedicated to manga, anime, and all facets of Asian pop culture. As the opening of the event loomed, Samantha worked tirelessly to get her comics ready. But printed comics were not this teenager's sole focus of the convention. Samantha practiced "cosplay," short for "costume play." She dressed as her favorite characters, planning a different character with appropriate outfits and apparel for each day of the convention. Samantha considered two distinct appearances of herself as the character Lenalee Lee from the series *D.Gray-Man* by Katsura Hoshino.[1] In one version, she would appear with short hair, bandages, and special pouches while the other featured her in a dress, but she could choose the latter outfit only if she was able to find someone to curl her hair the right way. Samantha even brought on an "assistant" to help her prepare for the convention. This unnamed (and certainly unpaid) friend kept track of what Samantha needed to accomplish before the convention, worked on her hair for certain cosplay styles, and even reminded Samantha to eat if she became too involved in her artwork.

Samantha connected with the larger world of manga through her blog, which has received over seven thousand page views since she launched the site in the summer of 2007. The blog was a combination of image galleries and written entries that related Samantha's ideas about manga alongside hundreds of art uploads from her sketchbooks and MLKHS publications. Samantha provided regular updates about the progress of her manga, informing readers about difficulties she was having with a certain character, for example, or conveying her excitement about finishing a piece. Readers responded with feedback—words of encouragement when Samantha seemed cheerless and extensive praise for newly uploaded art.

Aside from being a portal to Samantha's extensive manga output, however, the blog was also Samantha's public diary. Her entries included complaints about her chronic back pain, conflicted thoughts about relationships with boys, annoyance at having to babysit her cousins, postings on the status of her deteriorating computer, and a variety of other topics, many of them extremely personal. She wrote about abusive relationships, about her therapist, about the intricacies of her private life. More than a few readers were concerned when Samantha wrote that she considered "quitting" life. They posted responses that indicated how important Samantha's work was to them, even though they had never met in person. Their words inspired Samantha to forge on.

Samantha nearly dropped out of MLKHS when a strained relationship with her parents came to a head, and she became a minor on her own in New York City. Although she eventually returned home, the relationship with her family never fully recovered. In her blog she often described the violence in the household—broken furniture and smashed dishes that resulted from fights, bruises, occasionally blood on the floor that she had to mop clean. As a punishment for her perceived rebelliousness, adults in Samantha's life forbade her to attend the comic book club for an extended time, which she described as one of the darkest periods in her life.

Even with all this, Samantha nearly graduated from MLKHS in four years but was a few credits short. She returned in the summer to complete the requirements and obtain a diploma. Once she turned eighteen, Samantha sought desperately to move out of the house, but she did not have the financial resources. The search for a job, roommate, affordable housing commenced. She planned to go to college, but her late graduation forced her to defer enrollment until her life became settled. In the face of all the adversity at home and school, however, Samantha continued creating her manga and even increased the quantity and quality of her output in the most stressful times. She simply had to make manga, for the sake of her own existence and that of the online fans who celebrated her work. It seemed as though hardships that Samantha faced fed her desire to succeed as a *mangaka*, every challenge another bridge crossed on the road to independence.

Gallery Notes

Samantha's manga is titled "Sama's Misadventures: Anime Con Blues." Even though she situates herself as the main character of the comic book, the story is not built on personal experience. She crafts the tale from a humorous occurrence that a friend of hers suffered at an anime convention. That said, the character embodies many aspects of Samantha's life. Along with a love of "J-rock" and "J-pop" (Japanese rock and pop), this teenage character practices cosplaying. She first introduces herself donning a ponytail and collared shirt. In cosplay, however, she sports highly stylized hair and a fashionable sweater with cut sleeves. Very much in the manga style, the transition between the two characters is bridged by humor. Samantha holds a deadpan expression as she supports a sign with an arrow pointing to her cosplay alter ego; the caption reads: "Insert flashback now." The flashback recalls a momentous day in the girl's life—the opening day of her first anime convention. One can imagine the hours that she primps for the event and deliberates on which character to employ as the basis of her cosplay. Surely, she spends days designing and perfecting her costume; she reviews her collection of manga and anime to get the look of the character just right; she consults with friends—other cosplay practitioners—on the details of her accessories. Now the exhilarating day has arrived.

Samantha's reverie is interrupted by someone calling her name. She turns to find another cosplayer, this one appearing as a *bishounen*. This type of male character with feminine characteristics is popular in manga, especially among young girls. The "beautiful boy" knows Samantha, presumably from her blog and published manga. He is glad to have found her early in the convention and wants to show her around the convention hall. Samantha is swept off of her feet. She describes him as a "real gentleman" as he escorts her through the maze of manga and anime vendors. The two become close. Samantha puts her head on his shoulder as they take a "cutesy" picture. Even their outfits match—Samantha turns the black trim of her costume from the first page of the manga to white, like the boy's, on the second page. It appears as though Samantha has found the love of her life within the first minutes of the convention. A small figure in the back of her conscience warns her otherwise, however: "Dearie, he's only cosplaying." The caution goes unheeded. This manga fanatic of a teenager, who in real life has such difficulty finding a boyfriend who shares her interests, finally has a soulmate. In Samantha's mind, he and she will share their lives together by traveling to anime conventions and wowing the crowds with their character likenesses, not to mention their devotion to each other as cosplaying soulmates.

The humor and irony of the story surface in the third page. The *bishounen* suddenly doubles over with agonizing pain. Samantha exhibits concern for her new boyfriend. He assures her that he will be alright: "Just having some cramps . . . It sucks to be biologically female!" Samantha smiles at first, then explodes with a classic comic book double-take. Her hairdo comes undone, eyes turn white, cheeks become pink, and mouth transforms into a boxed grin of disbelief. Lines extend from the top of the panel, indicating the static in Samantha's mind. The word "ZING" appears between the lines, a verbal sting to Samantha's heart. The demure "oh" of the previous panel expands to an exasperated "OH?!" as Samantha comes to realize her mistake. She writes in a boxed caption: "That kind . . . gentlemanlike *bishounen* . . .was really a she . . .darn it life . . ." The image of Samantha—devoid of color, clasping the hand of the girl whom she previously thought to be a beautiful boy—is striking. A hollow laugh emanates from Samantha's mouth as her soul floats from her body into the air. The former *bishounen* begs for Samantha to continue to think of him as a male.

This scene highlights the important roles that androgyny and transgender identities play in manga culture and in the lives of the most ardent manga fans. Samantha's attraction to the *bishounen* at the convention is based on his delicate physical features and sensitive mannerisms, all socially accepted elements of a female person. Yet once Samantha gathers that the character is actually a girl, her heart is broken. These feminine attributes of male characters are prevalent throughout manga and may have roots in ancient Japanese culture. *The Tale of the Genji* by Lady Murasaki Shikibu from the eleventh century tells the story of a young prince with transcendental beauty that attracts both men and women.[2] The concept behind *bishounen* in modern manga is similar—the beauty of the boy transcends sex. His angelic and unmarred beauty is such that men and women alike are so engrossed that they forget about sex entirely. It is possible that a teenager like Samantha is enamored of the concept of *bishounen* and the manga in which they appear because sex has been extracted from the storyline. More likely, however, Samantha and the many other cosplayers in her world are experimenting with the boundaries of gender stereotypes in their lives and in society. Samantha has gone to great lengths to conceal her own gender in certain costumes while portraying specific characters, occasionally becoming a *bishounen* herself.

Samantha's comic concludes with the moral of the story, a lesson lost on a person unfamiliar with manga. She states: "So . . . I've learned that *bishounen* at anime cons may, in fact, not even be a *shounen* . . ." In other words, an attractive male teenager at an anime convention may not even be an immature young boy. Samantha considers *shounen* manga, with its sports, action, and fighting, to be representative of juvenile boys. And what about the girl cosplaying as a *bishounen*? Samantha reports: "He is in basic training for the Air Force." She makes a point of describing the person as "he," a testament to the girl's success at cosplaying. Samantha provides a portrait of the girl, now in glasses, a collared shirt, and something of a sly smile on her face. A tiny heart springs from the girl's shoulder, indicating Samantha's continuing adoration of the *bishounen* who once captured her own heart.

Chapter Ten

Tenzin

TENZIN WAS ONE OF THE FEW ASIAN STUDENTS at MLKHS and the only who participated in the comic book club during the course of this study. The personal trait that most embodied Tenzin was his quietness. He almost never spoke. While other club members shouted, laughed, and gossiped throughout the Thursday afternoon sessions, Tenzin huddled over his workspace and created comics in silence. Phil asked him about the progress of his work; Tenzin responded with a nod. A fellow club participant approached him for advice on an inking technique; Tenzin shrugged and pointed his chin toward the example that Phil had outlined on the whiteboard. Tenzin went to great lengths not to speak. On the days that I observed the club and interviewed students around the room, Tenzin left for the restroom or his locker just before I approached his spot at the table. When other adult visitors came to the club, Tenzin hunched over his drawings behind the dusty flatbed scanner as all the other students offered formal presentations of their comics. He often wrote answers to spoken questions on paper, and he occasionally drew his responses in quick sketches. I was finally able to ask Tenzin about the main character in the comic book he was developing—Tenzin drew a simple face with a tear in the corner of the eye. I had assumed that Tenzin's lack of verbalization resulted from either a language barrier or a speech impediment. When I learned of his background, I realized neither was the case.

Tenzin was born at the base of the Himalaya Mountains in Dharamsala, India, where he lived with his family alongside thousands of other Tibetan exiles. Tenzin's father worked as a soldier in the Indian army and a bodyguard for the Dalai Lama, but when money became scarce, the family was forced to place six-year-old Tenzin in a Tibetan Children's Village school. These schools were established across India shortly after the Chinese government forced the Dalai Lama and his followers to flee from Tibet into nearby India in 1959. While the mission of the Tibetan Children's Village had been to care for orphans and newly arrived children from Tibet, the organization became the lone educational institution for most Tibetan refugee children. Hence, in Dharamsala, headquarters of the banished Tibetan government and the Dalai Lama himself, thousands of Tibetan children flooded the schools. Tenzin was one of the many, a voiceless youth dazed by the separation from his parents and the dirty faces of countless other unkempt children all around him. He was assigned an identification number and led to living quarters that consisted of two bedrooms, each with twenty-five boys. They slept in makeshift bunk beds that reached to the ceiling. Needless to say, food and resources were scarce.

It was not until Tenzin turned fourteen that his family was able to collect enough money to flee the dire conditions in India and enter the United States. Tenzin enrolled at MLKHS and learned English quickly by sticking to the rule of thumb that guided his childhood in the refugee village: succeed in school or be tossed into the streets. He found his "voice," however, in the comic book club. Tenzin had never experienced comic books before, but Phil recognized the quiet teenager's affinity for making art and invited him to join the group. Tenzin was immediately drawn to the medium's combination of visual and literary features, the occasion to intertwine words with pictures. More significantly, Tenzin found in comic books an outlet for his ideas and opinions, which had never been heard, let alone valued, among the overwhelming glut of youths trying to survive as Tibetan refugees. His first comic book was about a man—"a regular guy like you and me"—who contracts AIDS from a prostitute. On the verge of suicide, the man finally finds solace in the one person from whom Tenzin himself retrieved unabated support—his father. Doing everything he could to save pennies for nine years in order to bring his family to the United States, Tenzin's father finally saw his dream realized. He came to the United States in 2000 and sent for the rest of the family in 2002. Tenzin was not oblivious to the magnitude of his father's sacrifices for the betterment of his family. Therefore, his first comic book became as much a tribute to his father as to Tenzin's new opportunities to voice ideas and beliefs, whether spoken or otherwise.

Despite holding a job in construction, working toward his high school diploma, and helping to support his family monetarily and emotionally, Tenzin was wholly committed to the comic book club. The other students respected him for his dedication, and they came to understand how he preferred to communicate—through art and writing. The comic books that Tenzin created established a bond between the Tibetan refugee and his fellow students at MLKHS. At first glance, these adolescents seemed to have little in common. They had distinct native languages, dissimilar cultures, and contrasting skin colors. However, the words and images in their comic books bridged the physical mountains and cultural experiences that separated them. Tenzin yearned for the other participants in the club to understand that he was neither Chinese nor Korean like the other Asian people that they had encountered; he was Tibetan, a people under siege and in need of help. Tenzin encouraged his fellow club mates to learn about his Tibetan culture, Buddhist religion, and mountainous homeland. In the process, they learned about Tenzin as a human being.

Through Tenzin, his friends became interested in aspects of their own cultures—not just as Latinos but as Colombians or Venezuelans, not just as African Americans but as Jamaicans or Haitians. He also helped them to value the importance of performing well in school. Tenzin formed a diverse study group whose members assisted each other in preparing for tests and securing good grades. His efforts were rewarded. Tenzin earned a scholarship to City College from the New York chapter of the United Federation of Teachers. He planned to use the scholarship to become a doctor. He wanted to help children like himself when he was young, those who struggle to maintain healthy bodies and minds when it would be easier to surrender to hopelessness. Tenzin aimed to live his life as an example of how far hope can take a person.

Gallery Notes

Tenzin's one-page story about the plight of Tibet represents his lifelong commitment to a faraway homeland and his ongoing efforts to see the end of oppression for his people. This piece also signifies the extent to which Tenzin maximizes the comic book medium as a form of communication, especially in contrast to his reluctance to converse. No other club participant exploits the page like Tenzin, filling every corner with ink in order to convey his message. His use of a single page is deliberate. Tenzin hopes that people will post this page as a flyer, distribute it as a leaflet, hold it up to cameras during a freedom march for Tibet. More than a political statement, Tenzin's work is a call to action. He approaches the comic as he would a persuasive essay, establishing a thesis and then supporting his argument with facts and data. The tactic engages the reader in the essential issues related to the history of Tibet and the enduring conflict between Tibet and China, at least according to Tenzin. The divergence from a persuasive essay, however, is that the facts and data in Tenzin's comic are illustrated with distinct colors, varied panel shapes, and multiple perspectives embedded in the visual imagery. Those unfamiliar with the nature of the Tibetan conflict not only experience Tenzin's passion about the subject but also feel persuaded to take up his cause.

The page begins with an idyllic image of Tibet's snowcapped mountains, green fields, and flowing rivers of fresh water. Tenzin describes Tibet as "the roof of the world" because of the region's high altitude. In the first panel, Tenzin dots the serene landscape with tents and yaks, which he features in greater detail in the second panel. We begin to understand the extent of Tenzin's knowledge of Tibet. He lists the three regions of the country—Amdo, Kham, and U'tsang—and explains that the nomads live in tents because they travel the countryside by yak. Tenzin highlights a nomad in traditional Tibetan clothing; he pointed out to me that the *chuba* shirt keeps the nomad warm in the winter, the boots are soft and flexible, and the woolen hat features a traditional colorful streamer so that others can spot the nomad in the field. Continuing to describe the natural beauty of Tibet, Tenzin introduces the panda, "one of the most beautiful and rare animals in the world." Peaceful and undisturbed, the panda chews on bamboo with mountains and waterfalls in the background. Tenzin makes use of the beauty of Tibet to lull the reader into a sense of stillness and harmony; he portends what is to come with a simple statement: "Pandas are harmless."

The sudden insertion of political upheaval into the comic is as surprising as the Chinese invasion that Tenzin describes: "In 1959, Chinese troops started taking over Tibet. They had planned it 10 years before." In contrast to the array of colors representing the natural beauty of Tibet, Tenzin introduces the Chinese soldiers in solid green uniforms against a brown background of dust and dirt. An army truck spews exhaust into the air. The invasion is in full force, and Tenzin depicts Tibetan people with sticks and spears attempting to defend themselves from the army soldiers with guns. Tenzin uses facts from his research to explain how the population imbalance added to the difficult situation: "Some tried to fight back but they failed due to sheer numbers. Tibet had only six million people versus China who had 700 million people at 1949–1959." In Tenzin's re-creation of the incursion, he shows laughing Chinese soldiers murdering defenseless Tibetans on their knees, pleading not for mercy but for a free Tibet. As Tenzin draws the stream of blood and colors it red, he relives the sacrifice of the many Tibetans who died in the violence.

The most harrowing image of the comic is that of snow-covered mountains backed by a sunny sky in the middle of the page. Tenzin spreads tiny black dots across the mountains, perhaps yaks, as he seemingly returns to the tranquil nature landscape. His text informs us otherwise: "These tiny dots represent humans on the mountains. They are trying to escape the Chinese army. Most died on the way because it's too cold and there's not enough oxygen to breathe." The palace where the Buddha and Dalai Lama once resided is now deserted. The pandas are caged and carted off in another polluting truck similar to the one that deployed the Chinese troops at the beginning of the assault. The yaks are slaughtered. The temples and monasteries are destroyed by heavy artillery. Tenzin is specific about how the Chinese torture the Tibetans: He portrays a Tibetan citizen hanging from his feet as a Chinese soldier ruthlessly thrashes the man.

Tenzin ends the comic with a statement of alarm and a shout of defiance: "These crimes are still going on to this day in 2004! FREE TIBET NOW!" He wants to move readers to action by highlighting the injustices that he has experienced along with those that he has learned from research and family members. In small writing on the side of the page, Tenzin repeats the cry to "Free Tibet!!" and provides two websites where readers can obtain more information. In providing these information sources, Tenzin hopes that readers will become passionate about Tibet and do what they can to help. He had an outlet in the comic book club where his mode of communication could be read and seen and where his voice—whatever form it takes—could be heard.

TIBET WAS A VERY PEACEFUL, QUIET PLACE WITH NO WAR. IT IS KNOWN AS "THE ROOF OF THE WORLD." THERE ARE THREE PARTS OF TIBET (AMDO, KHAM AND U'TSANG)

THIS NOMAD LIVES IN A TENT. HE DOESN'T NEED TO BUILD A HOUSE BECAUSE THEY TRAVEL PLACE TO PLACE BY YAK. YAK IS A BEAUTIFUL ANIMAL FROM TIBET.

PANDAS ARE ONE OF THE MOST BEAUTIFUL AND RARE ANIMALS IN THE WORLD.

IT EATS BAMBOO AND OTHER PLANTS. PANDAS ARE HARMLESS.

IN 1959, CHINESE TROOPS STARTED TAKING OVER TIBET. THEY HAD PLANNED IT 10 YEARS BEFORE.

THEY KILLED MANY TIBETAN PEOPLE. SOME TRIED TO FIGHT BACK, BUT THEY FAILED DUE TO SHEER NUMBERS. TIBET HAD ONLY SIX MILLION PEOPLE VERSES CHINA WHO HAD 700 MILLION PEOPLE AT 1949 - 1959. WE DIDN'T HAVE WEAPONS LIKE GUNS TO FIGHT AGAINST THEM.

HA HA HA HA

FREE TIBET! AMAH AH

THIS IS THE PALACE WHERE OUR GOD AND OUR COUNTRY PRESIDENT LIVED IN THE CENTER OF THE CITY OF LHASA.

MOUNTAINS SURROUND TIBET. THESE TINY DOTS REPRESENT HUMANS ON THE MOUNTAINS. THEY ARE TRYING TO ESCAPE THE CHINESE ARMY. MOST DIED ON THE WAY BECAUSE IT'S TOO COLD AND THERE'S NOT ENOUGH OXYGEN TO BREATHE.

PANDA 卫 子
CHINESE

THA!

HA HA

THEY CAPTURED THE ANIMALS. THEY KILLED MANY PANDAS AND YAKS.

THEY BEAT THE TIBETAN PRISONERS WITH WHIPS AND TIED UP THEIR HAIR WITH HEAVY ROCKS.

THEY DESTROYED ALL THE TEMPLES AND MONASTARIES.

THESE CRIMES ARE STILL GOING ON TO THIS DAY IN 2004!

FREE TIBET NOW!

Chapter Eleven

Reggie

REGGIE HELD A WIDE RANGE OF INTERESTS: comedy, screenwriting, stage plays, dancing, martial arts, and creative writing were near the top of the list. His main expressive outlet, however, was designing manga. He was avid in his endorsement of manga over American comics. According to Reggie, American comics rehashed the same characters many times over. He quickly tired of reading about Superman's next good deed, which reminded him of the feat before and the one prior to that. The repackaging of an "ultimate" Spider-Man or a "young" X-Men made Reggie feel like he had wasted his money on comics reshaped from those already in his collection. The string of blockbuster movies based on comics books solidified Reggie's opinion that the era of American comics had passed; the movies delivered the classic characters and stories in a neatly packaged two-hour feature, firmly sealing the caskets of dead superheroes that Reggie renounced for manga. For Reggie, manga featured an endless flow of characters, themes, extensions, and variations that awakened his creative sensibilities. Reggie believed that if political leaders were to read some of his favorite manga—those set in barren wastelands on a future earth, for example—they would come to realize the long-term and irreparable damage wreaked by wars and environmental neglect. Reggie truly believed that manga could save the world.

Reggie took pleasure in crafting manga warriors who were also protectors, who never sacrificed their morals or shirked their responsibilities in the face of life's most daunting challenges. He explained that his desire to create such characters was an extension of his troubled life out of school. His mother was in an abusive relationship that Reggie and his sister had witnessed throughout their childhoods. When the family finally broke free, they moved from his grandmother's house to a shelter to another relative and back to his grandmother. Reggie's mother, physically and psychologically damaged, often could not decide when to move or where to go; Reggie became the decision maker for the family. His loving but misguided mother spent her meager paychecks on toys and games for the children. It was fun at the time, Reggie recalled, but the family would certainly pay later for these extravagances with outstanding utility bills and persistent creditors.

Reggie's comics were both a reflection of this reality and an escape to an alternate universe where he controlled the inputs and outcomes. He transformed friends and family members into manga characters and incorporated aspects of their lives into the storylines. In his comics, Reggie lived by the rule of the samurai—he fought for justice and respect with a combination of personal convictions and sharp swords. His enemies were evil but reasonable. They respected Reggie for his physical and moral strengths. When he defeated them, which he always did, the foes felt as though they had been beaten by a virtuous warrior. Outside the world of his comics, however, Reggie was not so optimistic about the future. He saw his extended family fall into petty crime and drugs. He believed that his peers at school were wasting their lives as clones, falling prey to mass-marketing campaigns for unnecessary products and fulfilling stereotypes as violent criminals and drug users. Reggie wished that the people in his life could find inspiration in manga, where the characters were never perfect but always compassionate. He believed that manga could teach others about morality, loyalty, empathy, and the consequences for one's actions—all the things that Reggie felt would be necessary for people to improve their lives, whether transcending poverty, turning away from substance abuse, or relinquishing an abusive relationship.

Reggie described himself as a "popular loser" in school. He was considered a friend by many of his peers because he had a sense of humor and never pretended to be anything that he was not. Yet he also exhibited what he considered to be unpopular traits, especially his fondness for making art. A number of well-liked students at MLKHS bullied those who acted or dressed differently, and more often than not those victims turned out to be artists, according to Reggie. Reggie tried to protect his fellow artists who were being harassed. He told bullies: "You don't know what that kid is going through, so don't laugh." Reggie admitted, however, that on occasion he caught himself making fun of students, once mocking a boy in the hallway for his unabashed impression of the comic-book character Wolverine. Reggie cut short his ridicule, realizing the extent to which his favorite manga characters had personally impacted his own life. Reggie never wanted to be a hypocrite. He was aware of the irony that surrounded the high school pecking order. Those students who were considered the losers in high school often turned out to be the winners in life, the ones who started businesses, directed movies, or created new fashions. More than anything, Reggie wanted to be one of those people.

For this reason, Reggie felt cheated by MLKHS. While other adolescents somewhere else in the world were receiving a quality education and preparing for careers, Reggie was stuck in what he considered dead-end classes with students who did not care about their own futures. He was angry that the school offered art for only a few semesters and did not foster his creative interests through scholarships or internships. He considered transferring to one of the "upscale" art-oriented high schools like LaGuardia, but he found the system impossible to navigate. After reviewing the heap of forms and required transcripts and portfolios, Reggie decided to stick with MLKHS and devote as much time as he could to making comics. In some ways, he was satisfied with this decision; it prepared him for the life challenges he would certainly face as a professional artist. He would be surrounded by "haters," people who would scoff at his work out of jealousy or resentment. As an artist, Reggie would have to make his own way, just as he forced himself to do at MLKHS.

Gallery Notes

Reggie's comic book, "Twilight Odyssey," is the start of an ongoing series with dozens of samurai heroes, villainous rogues, interplanetary settings, and complex plot twists. As is common in manga, he devotes the first page to introducing the scenario, beginning with the evil "Snakelings" and the four "ultraga shards" hidden within the realms of the world. A science fiction story at heart, "Twilight Odyssey" highlights Reggie's ability to communicate through art and writing the array of ideas in his mind. His drawn image of the Snakelings is harrowing, all the more so considering his accompanying text: "These creatures are fused with snakes of all kinds. They drain life energy throughout the world's realms." The forces at play in Reggie's comic are intertwined with the social and political issues of the day, thereby forcing readers to consider the impacts of every character's actions. Hence, these villains do not simply land on earth and destroy humankind. Rather, the Snakelings aim to take control of the mystical shards that power the elements of water, earth, fire, and air, "the delicate balance of our fragile planet." Reggie introduces the main villain—half his scarred face peeking into the cloud of floating shards. His striking description of the villain as "a resurrected evil" reveals another strength of Reggie's comic—his confident experimentation with language.

Of course, the yet-unnamed villain and his Snakeling minions do not go unopposed. A hero stands in their way. Sion Dragonheart is a sword-wielding, African American samurai with a posse of likeminded friends. Reggie provides an image gallery for the sidekicks, each with a visual profile and a name. The sidekicks are not all human—a catlike creature named Sheridgia is featured in the middle of the gallery. The comrades, and the readers, are introduced on the next page to the Ruler of the Snakelings, King Devlorn. Reggie depicts King Devlorn with bleached white skin, a noticeable contrast to the dark tones of Sion Dragonheart. The snake monster stands before a smoky red background and brandishes an enormous, twisted spear. At first, King Devlorn appeals to Sion's sense of uprightness: "You know, Sion, we are not so different, you and I! We've both lost something precious to us, and both our destinies intertwine in a way that affects the people around us!" Reggie is helping readers build a context for King Devlorn, perhaps setting the stage for a prequel comic book that focuses on this dastardly ruler of the Snakelings and how he came to be so malevolent.

Villain that he is, King Devlorn does not remain affable. He taunts Sion, warning him that his "pathetic story" is about to end. Moreover, Devlorn tells Sion that he wishes the hero could have seen "the look on Patricia's face when I blasted her in the back!" Reggie pays tribute to two people in this scene: Patricia, who helped oversee the comic book club, and his grandmother, one of the few stable family members in his life. The jagged edge of the cartoon bubble at the end of the second page highlights Sion's rage. Once Sion learns that King Devlorn is responsible for the murder of his grandmother, the tension builds. With his fist in the air and his body surrounded by a blazing yellow and red aura, Devlorn continues his jeering: "Realize the full power of what darkness can do! Only then you might have a chance to defeat me or else fail and disgrace your 'granny' . . ." Reggie propels the story into high action through a span of imagery—Sion's foot launching from the ground, Devlorn's furrowed brow. The battle is about to begin, but not before Sion speaks his mind: "All of you so-called villains are so alike! None of you understand anything about life!" Each warrior unsheathes his sword; they meet face to face with intense stares between them. Reggie plays with a number of different angles and perspectives, giving the reader an unsettled sense of angst over the hero's prospects in the battle certain to follow. Will Sion avenge the death of his grandmother? Will King Devlorn and the Snakelings abscond with the four elemental ultraga shards?

The battle ensues on the next page. Reggie begins the sequence with a close-up of Sion's weapon. The "click" implies that the weapon has broken into two, perhaps indicating the demise of Sion after all. We learn otherwise in the next panel, which features a panoramic image of the hero and his pair of glowing swords. "I'll make you understand!" shouts Sion. This statement encapsulates everything that Sion hopes to achieve in battle: saving the earth from evil, taking revenge for the violent death of his grandmother, forcing a villain to value human life. This statement also summarizes what Reggie, the author, expects to accomplish with his comic book; he will make readers understand the passion of his art and words. He wants them to know that his comic book is important to him and that the hours he spent creating this work were valuable in his eyes. As the swords clash and the forces of good and evil collide, it is the author who eventually succeeds. Reggie shares his world of samurai fighters caught in the struggle to save the world from reptilian evildoers. He allows his imagination to run free and then harnesses those ideas in a display of literary and artistic self-exploration. Through the story of an evil snake king and a sword-bearing hero, Reggie took a step closer to understanding his own identity as a creative artist and writer.

PROFILE THE SNAKELINGS:

Twilight Odyssey

BY REGINALD

SNAKELINGS ARE BEINGS CREATED BY THE ENERGY OF THE ANTI-ULTRAGA SHARD. THESE CREATURES ARE FUSED WITH SNAKES OF ALL KINDS. THEY DRAIN LIFE ENERGY THROUGHOUT THE WORLD'S REALMS. THIS INCREASES THEIR STRENGTH AND POWER. THEY HAVE EXISTED FOR THOUSANDS OF YEARS THEY ARE THE SWORN BLOOD ENEMIES OF THE DRAGONS.

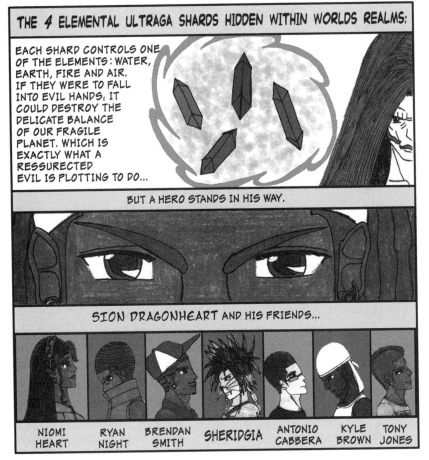

THE 4 ELEMENTAL ULTRAGA SHARDS HIDDEN WITHIN WORLDS REALMS:

EACH SHARD CONTROLS ONE OF THE ELEMENTS: WATER, EARTH, FIRE AND AIR. IF THEY WERE TO FALL INTO EVIL HANDS, IT COULD DESTROY THE DELICATE BALANCE OF OUR FRAGILE PLANET. WHICH IS EXACTLY WHAT A RESSURECTED EVIL IS PLOTTING TO DO...

BUT A HERO STANDS IN HIS WAY.

SION DRAGONHEART AND HIS FRIENDS...

| NIOMI HEART | RYAN NIGHT | BRENDAN SMITH | SHERIDGIA | ANTONIO CABBERA | KYLE BROWN | TONY JONES |

Chapter Twelve

Treasure

TREASURE FIRST CAME RELUCTANTLY to the comic book club when a friend dragged her there. Her friend was interested in manga, but Treasure was ambivalent. As her friend dabbled in some pencil sketches and managed a few reproductions of popular manga characters, Treasure bided her time by chatting and gossiping with a circle of female club members as they designed their comics. She was not a nuisance like some of the intruders who rowdily burst into the clubroom on their way to basketball practice or tutoring, but she did not contribute much to the group at that point either. Through the influence of her friend, and in order to converse eruditely with others in the group, Treasure began to read some of the manga that passed her way. She opened to one of the pages out of curiosity, slowly navigating through the "backward" sequence of the Japanese comics translated into English. She read with more intent as the weeks passed, manga such as *Bleach*, *D.Gray-Man*, and *Godchild*.[1] She gabbed much less as the stories held her attention for entire club sessions. Eventually, Treasure's friend left the club; creating manga turned out to be too time-consuming for her. Treasure, however, remained.

When Phil first placed a pencil into Treasure's hand, she was hesitant to draw, afraid of making a mistake. It took some time for Phil to convince Treasure that mistakes were part of the process. He explained that mistakes were something to be valued as a learning experience. He showed her the multitude of other students' drafted comics, marred with smudge marks, eraser streaks, written notes in the margins. Treasure was skeptical, but she did eventually put her pencil to paper. She began to compose characters from the manga that she had learned to enjoy reading. These early sketches appeared as doodles. Treasure drew the face of a character followed by some scribbles, then continued on with the body of the character in an entirely different section of the paper. Phil worked to help Treasure focus on complete drawings of original characters rather than recreations of published material. Just as with taking the risk of drawing at the outset, the concept of designing something unique and imaginative was intimidating to Treasure. Phil repeatedly insisted: "Do it your way!" But Treasure was unwilling. It seemed as though she would either persist with her random doodling or quit the club.

Phil exhibited patience, however, and eventually Treasure started to create original work. She showed a predilection for female characters with long, flowing hair and fair skin—sharp contrasts to her own physical appearance. She especially concentrated on her characters' eyes, establishing a particular sense of longing in one character and mystique in another. She also took great pains in the details of her characters' clothing—another dissimilarity to the teenager's simple t-shirts and jeans. Her manga creations wore dresses covered with frilly embellishments or shawls adorned with black buttons. Treasure designed a range of full-length female characters from an innocent bride with a bouquet of roses to a seductive, leather-clad vixen. She began to experiment with different inking techniques and a variety of colors that seemed to push the characters off the page and into the physical space before the eyes of the viewer. She developed a knack for teasing with angles in her artwork so that the characters appeared to move in a whirl of energy. It seemed clear that after much coaxing from Phil and encouragement from the other club members, Treasure had finally found her artistic stride.

Nevertheless, it took Treasure another leap of creative faith to plan and draft storylines that would eventually turn into comic books. Given all the complexities of the manga that she now read with extreme pleasure, Treasure never believed that she could write something captivating enough to hold a reader's attention. She considered herself proficient at writing, but the creative aspect of story development overwhelmed her. Having rarely experienced opportunities in school to pursue creative writing, Treasure balked at the thought of brainstorming ideas for a potential story. The plateau that she had reached with doodling had stretched to an even larger plateau in character designs. The weeks turned into months as Treasure continued to design characters without stories to match. The deadline for the culminating publication of 2007 approached, and Treasure could only offer one of her many character drawings, which appeared on a page near the back of the book.

Treasure's original manga stories began to surface in 2008 after she heeded the advice of a fellow club member: "Write about yourself." She had heard this counsel many times before, but she considered her life boring and could not imagine how her personal experiences might transform into a fantastical manga page-turner. Through the work of her peers, however, Treasure realized that the most complex manga, with mind-bending plot twists and a ceaseless flow of fresh characters, were actually simple tales at their core: love stories, adventures, fantasies. The characters experienced hardships, they learned about themselves and the world around them, they used their knowledge in future endeavors and journeys. Treasure began to consider her own hardships—ferocious arguments between her parents or a falling out with a friend. She found story fodder in her daily experiences by imagining a manga version of the same events. In this manner, the details of her life that she had considered the most mundane developed into realistic traits of the characters that appeared in her pages. The result turned out to be manga that simultaneously reflected Treasure's personal experiences and spoke to the parallel interests and experiences of her peers. This cohort of teens encouraged Treasure in her efforts to combine her dramatic artistic style with personal, humorous plots. Whereas the year before, Treasure had submitted a sole drawing for the final publication, in 2008 she produced a nine-page comic book, the longest ever to be published in an MLKHS compilation. Every page of this work highlighted Treasure's growth as an artist, but it was the story that kept the readers engrossed to the end of her manga. Considering that she began in the club as a tagalong, Treasure's accomplishments over the course of a few years were remarkable, and they inspired her to continue on as an original manga designer with a list of creative ideas to pursue the future.

Gallery Notes

Treasure's comic, titled *Shizuka* after her main character Shizuka Tsurugi, could have been pulled directly from the pages of a Tokyopop or Viz publication. The artwork and writing capture the whimsical nature of manga—eyes full of expression, hair spiked high, text fonts clearly reflecting the actions and emotions of intriguing characters. Forgoing the Photoshop coloring techniques employed by other club members, Treasure opts for black-and-white pencil drawings, subsequently inked with a variety of black pens and markers. Treasure embraced the skill of inking; the range of black and gray tones enhances the elements of character design, perspective, and atmosphere throughout the comic. The inking technique is one example of Treasure's abilities; the line drawings are another. With simple lines and shapes, Treasure creates a world of stylish characters that bump against floating signs and symbols representing the inner workings of the characters themselves. She designs broken hearts for a love-struck girl and white bones of voodoo for a magical demon. With each new panel, Treasure puts forth a work of art unto itself, all connected through the sequential narrative of Shizuka, a teenager with a major crush.

It is that story, alongside the dramatic artwork, that resonates with manga fans. Treasure begins with a crazed Shizuka, obsessed over a handsome *bishounen*. With her eyes wide and mouth agape in a trancelike state, Shizuka scratches at the boy's locker. The humor of the story emerges as Treasure inserts her own commentary of disbelief, arrows pointing to Shizuka: "That's our main character?" The boy, who appears suddenly, is equally miffed. He says to Shizuka in a cool tone: "Excuse me, you are physically abusing my locker." Shizuka stresses to a laughable extreme at the appearance of her crush. Her eyes go wild, and her mouth expands in a scream of "YAAAHHHH," which lines the bottom of the panel. Broken hearts in her wake, Shizuka flees.

In this first page of the manga, Treasure leads the reader to believe that Shizuka is insane. Her severe emotional outbursts and mad expressions indicate that Shizuka has literally gone crazy with love. At the start of the second page, however, we learn that she is just a typical, lonely teenager consumed by her yearning for a cute guy. Treasure depicts Shizuka sitting against a wall, her face now consisting of two simple dots for eyes. With her emotions spiraling around her like ghosts, dejected Shizuka thinks: "I wonder how many restraining orders he's going to file against me?!" She then declares her "official wish," the text in a box bordered by a formal ribbon: "I wish that someone would bring us together and not in a court room . . ."

Being that the story is a manga, the wish is granted, in this case by a quirky demon named Faye. This hooded character features two peaks on her head like a devil's horns, except that these crests are modish wisps of hair. Faye's outfit is also outlandishly chic. The pairs of question marks and exclamation points behind Shizuka symbolize her bewilderment. Faye is all business—she presents Shizuka with a contract releasing the demon world from all culpability related to a series of numbered items on a list. The first exculpation is from "death" and the last from "becoming a street performer." Number two on the list is exactly what Shizuka seeks: "Legions of fan-boys chasing you." Number ten is a personal reminder from Treasure to herself: "Failing to graduate on time." Though hesitant, perhaps from the current of ominous bones emanating from Faye's body, Shizuka agrees to sign the waiver. In the pages that follow, Faye presents Shizuka with a wrapped candy and instructions to eat it just before bedtime. At a climax of the story—will Shizuka eat the candy, and what will happen if she does?—Treasure inserts more dry humor when Faye forgets to collect her fee: "Oh well, this lackluster borderline sewer worthy comic is almost done (for now). Hopefully the readers will bear with us a little bit longer!" Shizuka eats the candy.

The result is an unremitting rush of male suitors who fall at Shizuka's feet. She is forced to fend them off with karate kicks. One embattled boy with a large lump on his head asks: "Does this mean we're not going out?" The amorous boys surround Shizuka in class, at lunch, in the gym. Treasure transforms the boys into hovering banshees, each with a heart in place of his face. Shizuka begs for the craze to end as Faye looks on with a wide, malicious smile. The one boy who does not pursue Shizuka, however, is the very individual whom she covets. She pulls together enough confidence to tell the target of her affection about her crush on him since junior high school. Unfortunately, he tells Shizuka that she is not her type and fancies someone else. Treasure provides a visual metaphor for Shizuka's devastation—an image of Pluto smashing into earth. The manga ends with a deflated likeness of Shizuka as the demon Faye sardonically reminds her: "Don't you worry about it! There are plenty out there who'd like to date you, Shizuka!" The stream of suitors continues unchecked. Treasure concludes with a lesson for all of her readers: "Maybe it's better to just be yourself sometimes!"

In her manga, Treasure modernizes a classic tale of young love gone awry and the long literary history of the love potion. Treasure's story puts a manga spin on the omnipresent theme. Her story is set in front of high school lockers, and the style reflects the modern cartoon elements of illustrated words and dialogue bubbles. Yet the most important modernization in Treasure's work is the vital role of female characters, an enduring and important aspect of manga. It is a girl who takes the magic candy and a girl who gives it to her. The boys swoon over Shizuka, and she physically stops them with a powerful kick. And although Shizuka is smitten with a boy, female author in Treasure tells other girls to be themselves. Treasure takes up manga as a tool for developing powerful female characters, who in turn convey influential messages to countless female readers in her school and online around the world. Female manga characters may be important, but it is the female manga creators, like Treasure, who matter most.

Chapter Thirteen

Kischer

KISCHER WAS THE MOST SKILLED ARTIST to come through the comic book club at MLKHS. She was also one of the most at risk of a ruined life. In no uncertain terms, Kischer and school did not mix well. She was considered a "long-term absence" by the administration at MLKHS. When she did make an appearance, she was often in trouble for fighting, talking back to teachers, and numerous other infractions. As a result, Kischer's suspensions and academic probations distanced her from school to an even greater extent. On the days that Kischer passed through the metal detector into MLKHS, she sat in the back of her classes and drew. And drew and drew. As teachers lectured and introduced new topics, Kischer concentrated on nothing but the lead point of her pencil.

Those drawings—eye-popping to anyone who experienced them—were excruciatingly detailed portraits of mystical, often erotic, characters. The women in these images held distant gazes and were often bound by chains. Between the thousands of minuscule lines that comprised the illustrations, Kischer embedded skulls and skeletons, knives and skin mutilations. The connections between art and artist were not difficult to make. Kischer designed her pictures on book covers, the backs of assignment sheets, or in notebooks, where, of course, she was supposed to be taking notes. Frustrated teachers confiscated Kischer's drawings—she simply started afresh with another piece. A girl practically dead to everything else in the world, Kischer made art not just because it was the one thing at which she excelled but because it was the one thing that reminded her that she was alive.

Kischer eventually found her way into Phil DeJean's art room and tossed a pile of her drawings on his desk. Phil had never seen such advanced drawing skills demonstrated by a high school student; he was certainly impressed with what she presented. Yet after praising her, Phil did something that Kischer had never before experienced. He gave her criticism. He pointed out disproportions and irregularities in the hands of the figures that she had drawn, and he offered some ideas to help her improve. Kischer was stunned. It was not Phil's evaluation of "less than perfect" that dumbfounded her but the fact that he cared enough to take time to examine her artwork and talk with her about it. After lifelong negative experiences in school, Kischer never imagined that a teacher would support her, not even the art teacher. Kischer took Phil's two points of advice: (a) she focused on improving the design of her characters' hands, and (b) she began to attend the comic book club on Thursday afternoons.

Under Phil's guidance, and through the inspiration of other art-oriented students, Kischer became a core constituent of the club. The other club members were staggered by Kischer's art, but they also were able to communicate with Kischer about her process, techniques, pen weights, and content. They peered over her shoulder as her marker shaped designs; conversely, she learned from them about their steady work habits and commitment to manga design. Kischer began to read the manga strewn about the clubroom, and she promptly discovered an outlet for her abilities. She learned from her newfound friends the details of the manga business, the billions of dollars that flowed between consumers, publishers, and artists. The members of the group, including Kischer, figured that if they could obtain a piece of that pie—the tiniest of tiny slices—they could sustain themselves as professional manga creators. For the first time in her life, Kischer was able to envision a positive future for herself. She became aware of the linkages between visual art and not only comic books but also videogames, movies, cartoons, and websites, as well as advertisements, marketing campaigns, and logo designs. Somebody was making all of that art, and Kischer began to think that that somebody could be her.

Kischer became driven. She attended the club religiously. She communicated like a professional with Rebecca Fabiano, informing the director of what she hoped to accomplish through the comic book club. In response, Rebecca sought an internship opening for this once reticent, unpredictable teen, resulting in Kischer's cover design for a national publication of the Comic Book Project. I recall Kischer's face when I handed her the compensation check of fifty dollars—her eyes were bright with gratitude but also eager for more opportunities. The reward was more than monetary for her; it was a validation of the countless hours that she had spent in her life making art, when everyone around her was advising, instructing, demanding her to do something else. Kischer also began to take school more seriously. She realized the importance of a high school diploma in gaining employment as an artist. Her portfolio could not stand alone for most positions offered by a business or a corporation. However, Kischer had fallen so far behind in school that graduation seemed unattainable. At age seventeen, she had accumulated enough credits to be considered only a sophomore. Dropping out was a difficult decision for Kischer, especially considering the enthusiasm that she was just discovering for her future career. She elected to leave MLKHS, nonetheless. Still dubious of how her daughter could earn a living making art, Kischer's mother encouraged her to enter the federal Job Corps program and become a plumber's assistant.

Phil, on the other hand, convinced Kischer to pursue a GED. He assisted her in locating and registering for test preparation courses, and he aided her in studying for the exams. Kischer had learned from the comic book club how to establish a regimen and maintain it, which helped her stay on track with this new academic endeavor. All the while, Kischer continued to attend the comic book club, an exception granted to her by the Opening Doors program.

Her personal story highlights that, without question, a teacher can be a life-changing force, and a student—every student—has a pathway to success. Phil's advisement while Kischer attained her GED was only one facet of the close bond forged by these two artists. Phil and Kischer began to create comics together, Phil drafting the stories and Kischer designing the artwork. The collaboration proved successful, and eventually they embarked on a fantasy-based graphic novel about modern-day sorcerers. Kischer developed a multitude of characters for the work; Phil wove them into a story. They outlined the plot and storyboarded the sequence, and the book itself began to develop. Phil and Kischer hoped to design the book to completion in order to pitch it to publishers, animation companies, and movie studios. Kischer, who seemed destined for a life of disappointment, found herself creating a work that could transform her into the next celebrated graphic novelist.

Gallery Notes

"Ambika's New Job" is an example of a collaboration between Kischer and Phil. Kischer designed a coven of alluring witches, clothed (minimally) in leather bustiers and garters. Phil placed those characters in a plot based on the theme of teenage sexual relationships. Together they assigned personalities to the witches and led them through a story arc—introduction, conflict, and resolution. The main outline grew into a storyboard of pencil sketches and written notes. Phil and Kischer planned each panel by consulting with one another about the direction of the comic, determining how the characters would work toward the moral intended for the story. At the outset, Kischer focused almost exclusively on the artwork, drafting her witches as she sat at a table in the clubroom. Yet as the essence of the story came to light, she became more involved in the storyline. She offered ideas and suggestions for the flow of the narrative, the characters' dialogue, the nature of the captions. Phil predicted this would be the case, as he was aware of Kischer's personal investment in the theme of the comic book. As Phil suspected she would, Kischer became more than an artist in the collaboration; she took on the role of a dedicated coproducer.

"Ambika's New Job" begins with the witches flying about on their brooms, chatting as supernatural teenagers might on their way to a paranormal shopping mall. One flies above with a new "Lady K" broom model as the others drolly express their jealousy: "You are too cool for ghoul school!" The main character Ambika roars in with an animated "swoosh" and "smash," knocking her friends straight off their flying sticks. She announces the reason for her haste: "I gotta get over to my new job with a quickness!" Ambika has been hired as a grim reaper with the "Duppy Dispatch"—a crew of macabre skeletons who deal death to deserving humans. The skeletons mull about the dispatch room while drinking coffee and clocking in for another day on the job. Cloaks masking their bony frames, the skeletons sharply contrast with Ambika, the only witch—and only woman—in the office. One of the skeletons questions her ability to perform the job: "How can you work here, Ambika? You're a witch!" Ambika counters with an explanation of her bloodline—she is only half-witch. An affair with a handsome vampire during her "gothic phase" altered her forever. Clearly the relationship is something that Ambika does not enjoy discussing.

Ambika's job commences on the third page of the comic book. She sees before her two teenagers, a boy and girl. Their body language—the girl with her hands on her hips, the boy with one hand in his pocket and the other behind his head—indicates a confrontation. Ambika reminds herself: "I must be impartial, but I've got a feeling this guy has got it coming!" Her thumb points toward the scene. The comic book takes a violent turn as the teenage girl wields a hammer against the boy's head. Her rage is palpable as she screams: "That's for cheating on me with my own sister and getting her pregnant!" Downed and bloodied, the boy has yet to learn his lesson. As Ambika leans over his bruised body, he asks the witch out on a date. Ambika reaches to give him the touch of death, as her new job dictates. She says: "Sorry, Amigo! You've got a date with destiny!" The last image of Ambika, finger on her temple, reminds readers to think before they act. The moral of the story is highlighted in the last panel: "Lesson: Life is too short to be stupid! Messing around can cost you your life! Advice straight from the Duppy Dispatch!"

The influence of manga on Kischer's modern-gothic artistic style is evident throughout the story, especially in the hairstyles and the design of the eyes. The witch outfits similarly fit the seductive nature of many manga intended for adults. Phil's humorous writing style adds another aspect of whimsy to the work. However, when Kischer introduces the real-life relationship between the teenagers on the third page, she veers away from manga style. Rather than an androgynous *bishounen* for the boy, Kischer designs a muscular male wearing a tank-top and jeans. In place of the manga-specific garters and bustiers for the female character, Kischer dresses the girl in a simple skirt and halter-top. The contrast between the silliness of fantasized manga witches and the real-life circumstances of American teenagers comes to light in this portion of Kisher's comic book. Kischer, a teenager herself, aims for her readers to understand the severity of the situation related to teenage sex. This is a difficult state of affairs between two real people in New York City, not capricious Japanese constructs. Kischer is not shy in presenting exactly how devastating "messing around" can be—the girl is driven to a brutal assault on the boy who two-times her. Kischer returns to the manga-influenced Ambika at the very end of story, but the scene between the teenagers is a serious, if not extreme, reminder of the consequences of real-life decisions.

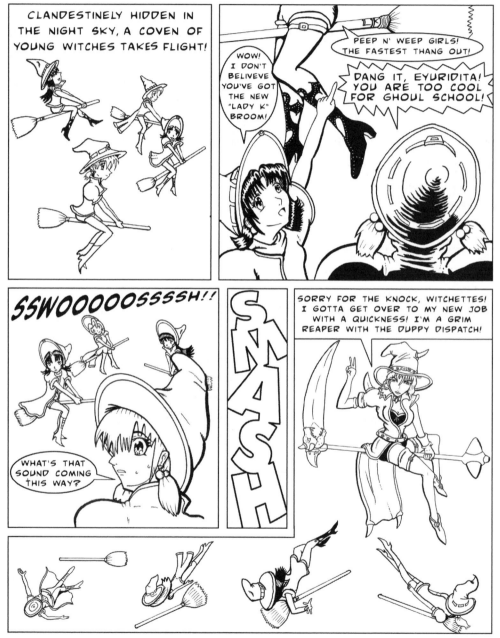

Chapter Fourteen

Keith

KEITH'S IS A PAINFUL STORY. Keith's mother was a hard drug user, blind or indifferent to the abuse that her boyfriend regularly inflicted on her young son. During one beating, Keith—slight and undernourished—found strength in his rage to retaliate. The young boy critically wounded the adult man. Keith subsequently began a staggering odyssey through the foster care system, passed from home to home in a cycle of abuse and hunger, anger and disillusionment. When he was forced to move on, Keith braced himself for the next horror.

At one particular home, Keith found himself locked in a room for hours. With only a paper and pencil at his disposal, Keith began to draw. The lonely boy's drawings formed into characters, and the characters began to interact. The characters looked on each other with love and hugged one another. They refrained from hitting and spitting. He wrote words over the characters' heads and eventually emanating from their mouths. The characters said kind things to each other; they spoke of wonderful places and fantasy worlds where violence never prevailed. Before long, Keith was designing comics, and the pastime to while away the hours in confinement quickly developed into a passion. The many villains in his life became villains in his comic books—monsters who went out of their way to harm innocent people. For example, Keith developed a comic book around a cyborg-ninja named Jack Snipe. Like Keith, Jack Snipe's mother takes up with an abusive boyfriend, and, like Keith, Jack Snipe is pushed too hard and is forced to fight back. Keith prominently portrays the man's fist and belt. He also depicts the weapon used for retribution.

In his subsequent stories, Keith became a hero named the Hunter, whom Keith described as "my dark persona, or at least how my persona would've been if I decided to go about solving my problems the angry and negative way." The relationship between Keith, the boy, and the Hunter, a comic book hero, developed differently. The Hunter was full of rage at the injustices in his life. Keith, too, was extremely angry because of his circumstances, but he learned how to channel that anger into his art and writing rather than vigilante violence. Part of his abstinence from retribution stemmed from a deathbed oath that Keith had made to his ailing grandfather: the boy would live a virtuous life no matter what ensued—a promise eerily similar to the central premises of prospective superheroes in so many comic book stories. Keith took the pledge so seriously that he abstained from cursing from that day on. Hence, whereas the Hunter wielded a deadly sword, Keith brandished a sharpened pencil that continually scratched out the story of a masked hero on the prowl for evil in the world. Keith believed in the power of karma, the idea of "what comes around goes around." For every villain that the Hunter hacked into pieces, Keith simply glowered at the real criminals in his life, sensing that they would eventually get what was due to them. Keith accepted whatever challenges that he faced as additional material for his comics, and he left the dirty work to the Hunter.

Keith entered MLKHS, however, not as the confident Hunter but as a confused adolescent still caught in the nightmare of transitional foster homes. He was an easy target for bullies at school, given his diminutive size, quiet demeanor, and limited selection of clothes. Keith quietly absorbed the taunts and inserted the bullies into his comics as fodder for the Hunter's quests for justice. Of course, pent-up anger, despite Keith's personal outlet, is unhealthy for any adolescent, and the deteriorating situation at school combined with the ongoing troubles at "home." They threatened to throw him from his self-directed disciplined path. Fortunately, he caught word of the formation of the comic book club, and was quickly on board. The club satisfied two important needs in Keith's life: (a) a community of peers with whom to share his creative ideas and comics, and (b) a way to stave off returning to whichever foster home that housed him in a given month. Keith found in the club a haven, the single place in the entire world where he could be at peace. Here he also met friends, like Reggie, who were just as avid about creating comics.

Under Phil's tutelage, Keith's skills as an artist and writer expanded rapidly. His work improved every week, likely because of the many hours that Keith spent honing his comics between club sessions. He relished Thursday afternoons, always one of the first in and last to leave. Along with developing more complex characters, Keith learned the value of perspective and angles in catching the reader's eye. His writing also improved dramatically. Keith began to incorporate words that he had gleaned from his favorite comic book series: "forsaken," bloodthirsty," "tranquility," "dimensional" to name a few.

Unlike most of the other members of the club, Keith had an affinity for American superhero comics as well as manga. Classic superheroes, including Spider-Man and the Hulk, established a moral grounding in his life. These characters were misunderstood and often reviled by the very citizenry that the heroes were trying to save. Keith sympathized with their plight, their need to "go it alone" because nobody in the world could possibly understand the nature of their problems. He was also strongly aligned with the superhero ethos of helping others in need; he believed strongly that if the individual in need stood within sight, one had an obligation to help. An independent among the comic book club members, Keith was wary of labeling his style as manga or classic American. He simply wanted as many people as possible to appreciate his work and, in turn, recognize him as a person with something important to contribute to the world.

The highlight of Keith's high school career was the one-week workshop at the Center for Cartoon Studies in Vermont, which he attended on scholarship in 2006. Rebecca and I were admittedly nervous at the idea of sending Keith. We were well aware of his unstable living situation, and Rebecca was unsure as to whether Keith was ready for the responsibility of representing the Opening Doors program. Yet he was most deserving of the award that year, and we agreed that a weeklong break from the city, and all the misfortunes that it held for him, could prove beneficial. During the week, he worked with professional cartoonists and comic book creators; they evaluated his work and established with Keith a long-term plan for bringing his comics to a professional level. Keith met other young comic book enthusiasts, who inspired him with their dedication to and knowledge about comics.

The boy who left New York City returned there as a young man with a mission: to become a professional comic book designer. He knew it would be a hard road, that many people would doubt him along the way. He wrote:

> For the most part, an artist's life is full of excitement, you always meet new people, you get to see things in a different light, your friends tend to be fun and goofy just like friends should be, none of that gang or thug stuff. You are always inspired by amazing art styles and stories and most of the time, you reach your goal one way or the other. Either you're Stan Lee's assistant or you own your own art company. Its just getting to your goal is always the hard part, but then if it wasn't everyone would be an artist and then you wouldn't stand out.

Keith started the next school year, his last at MLKHS, with an extremely positive attitude. His zeal for comics had only increased since the summer workshop, and the growth of his artistic and literacy skills matched his expanded enthusiasm. He inspired other club members to equal his work ethic, which consisted of not only attending the club every Thursday without fail but also entering the clubroom with a stack of completed pages ready for review and critique. Largely due to Keith's drive, the comics that the entire club produced at this time were unparalleled in terms of both quality and quantity. Keith was a quiet leader, demonstrating by example the extent to which determination could bolster a person's achievements. As a demonstration to new club members, Phil often compared Keith's new comics with his work from previous years. The difference was dramatic. Previously staid characters exhibited movement and emotion. Once-stagnant backgrounds became displays of detail and symbolism. Phil reminded the new recruits that only one explanation could account for Keith's transformation as a comic book creator: hard work. Keith was proud to be the example of success. He consistently offered praise and words of encouragement to his peers in the club, and they responded to his support with respect. Most satisfyingly, we began to observe Keith's frequent glowing smile.

But the comics club could not banish the real world. On his eighteenth birthday, Keith's foster parents no longer received monetary compensation for housing him and tossed him and his belongings onto the street. Their gift to him was a large garbage bag to carry his meager belongings. The one benefit that foster care had afforded Keith—a roof over his head—was no longer. In a matter of hours of turning eighteen, Keith became homeless and disappeared from school. When, out of desperation, he turned up again, Phil and Patricia witnessed a different Keith—the boy who had morphed into a young man only months before had now become a ghost: emaciated, dirty, battered by the cold and his lack of sleep. Phil immediately gave Keith a blanket, and Patricia bought him some food. They both encouraged him to come to them after school, and each day they provided him with food and money. Upon learning of his plight, I "hired" Keith through Teachers College so that he could collect a small paycheck. Patricia, Phil and the Opening Doors administrators also made sure that the proper authorities at MLKHS became aware of Keith's situation. The Administration for Children's Services was ultimately able to find Keith temporary housing and a small monthly stipend.

Through these truly difficult times, Keith continued making comics when he could, but his artistic endeavors and career plans took a backseat to survival. Patricia in particular attempted to counsel Keith and provide him with hope for the future. She encouraged Keith to continue with the graphic novel based on his life experiences as told through the story of the Hunter. She convinced him to participate in the plans for a documentary, which served the purpose of her meeting Keith every week at Teachers College so that she could monitor his health and well-being. At times, Keith would vanish for a week or two, but through her persistence, he eventually returned. Whenever she saw him again, she bought him food or gave him the few dollars in her wallet and, to the best of her efforts, guided Keith through the despondency that consumed his life. It is a wonder, in fact, that Keith never turned to the violent, destructive ways of the Hunter. Eventually, Keith returned to a semblance of the personality that we had come to know, although he never smiled quite as widely as he once did.

In the end, it would have been nice to report that Keith pulled through and followed his dreams of becoming a famous comic book artist. Unfortunately, his life continued to teeter. When I asked him to sign a form so that his artwork could be included in this book, he printed and signed his name with excitement. Over the address line, however, Keith simply wrote a question mark.

Gallery Notes

These three pages of "Legend of the Hunter" are Keith's prologue to a full-length comic book, perhaps even a graphic novel. They act as a curtain to be pulled on the story that unfolds in the many pages that follow—the tale of Hunter. This introduction sets the scene by establishing the central character: a sword-wielding hero, savior of some, terror to most. Equally important in these pages, Keith fashions an atmosphere of mystery and intrigue. None of the characters are shown in full; the narrator is represented by an empty chair near the fire. He speaks to a concealed daughter. The Hunter, our hero, is first depicted as a shadow. Keith portrays the Hunter's sword, then his menacing eye eclipsed by a dripping flow of blood. We see his muscular back as he kneels before the graves of "loved ones, best friends, and teammates." (Notice the Snipe family name on the gravestones featured on the second and third pages, a reference to his earlier comics endeavors.) The Hunter's face remains a mystery; Keith entices us to read on in order to catch a glimpse of the famed hero. His clues help us form our own mental images of who the Hunter is and what he looks like, but we cannot possibly know for certain until Keith decides it is time. In no uncertain terms, Keith is in power as he directs this comic book.

The words are also mysterious and menacing: "It is neither a happy tale nor a pleasing tale, but one I must tell nevertheless . . ." The Hunter stands "against the glow of a burning city," a "terrible land" with the villainous "corrupt souls." In the next panel, Keith dramatically switches from the expansive cityscape to a panel showing an extreme close-up of the Hunter's face. An inexperienced comic book creator might have considered the scene set and the story primed for an alien invasion or a bloody battle. But Keith continues to build a persona for the Hunter with a chilling description: the Hunter "moved swiftly and silently with a look of hate and strength in his eyes . . . It was not the bloodthirsty scowl of a reaper or the twisted look of a madman . . . It was the look of a man whose heart was filled with pain and sorrow. The look of a man who fights not for loved ones or morals but one who fights for himself! The look of a man driven to battle because he knows a secret. A secret that has left him with only the will to fight and a sense of honor . . ."

Most of the backgrounds in Keith's comic book are lightly shaded, so when he introduces the villain Chaos on a black canvas, the effect is striking. The cloaked figure is surrounded by flames—not red and yellow like the fires from the burning city but blue and purple. The face of the villain is masked; the whites of his pupils barely appear in the image. Just as with the Hunter, Keith aims to establish a context for Chaos: "It was said that the demon Chaos had killed the gods themselves and took their powers." Upon reading this and returning to the dance of dark flames that Keith has drawn, the reader becomes aware that Chaos is the embodiment of evil. Those flames of malice are contrasted in the final panel with the more familiar fire in the hearth. Keith concludes the prologue, telling us that the "night is cruel, and it will be a long time before the sun rises." The story is about to begin, so settle in for a literary ride.

The narrator of the story states: "I have also witnessed terrors beyond any description . . . but nothing in my whole life compares to him . . ." The Hunter, Keith's dark side, his rage, his ability to break—these were the nightmares that haunted Keith. Yet the acts of writing, drawing, and collaborating with others enabled Keith to synthesize the ongoing trials of his life and transform them into engaging literature. Even though Keith tells us in his prologue not to pray, we all yearn for the story not to end tragically.

Conclusion

Beyond the Comics

THE FUTURE OF THE COMIC BOOK CLUB at MLKHS is unclear. Phil and Rebecca are no longer with the program. Shonda Streete has kept the club alive so far, but faces the inevitable challenges of budget cutbacks and administrative reorganization. I wonder if the decision makers will recognize the academic and social implications of this high school comic book club. Perhaps while surfing the Internet, one of those decision makers will come across a manga posted by Samantha and will read the streams of comments celebrating her work as a masterpiece. Perhaps one of those people will meet Tenzin at a rally for Tibet, or perhaps in his future medical office, and learn how the club impacted his life as a student and an immigrant. Perhaps one of those people will meet Keith, exiting the storefront of his future comic book company, and learn how the club not only changed his life but saved it as well.

Whether or not those unlikely encounters ever happen, the youths at MLKHS, like their peers around the world, continue to read and design manga. The comics continue to represent the urban youths' ideas, hopes, fears, dreams, and identities. With each new manga, the teenagers' writing and art is more imbued with reflections of themselves and stories about the city in which they live, yet their work still maintains the delicate intricacies of the Japanese medium now so integral a component of their own cultures. There is no guarantee that manga will continue to impact young people to this extent, or to any extent, in the future. However, for these youths during these years at MLKHS, these comic books have come to define the lives of some dedicated young readers, writers, and artists.

Educational Implications

Despite the MLKHS students' enthusiasm for manga and comics, the most important aspect of this book is neither manga nor comics. Rather the core concept here is the students' enthusiasm—the excitement and discipline with which the students approach the self-initiated task of writing and designing comic books. They have chosen this pursuit. They would find ways to create manga with or without the comic book club, the Opening Doors program, MLKHS, teachers, principals, boards of education, or graduation diplomas. It just so happens that this passion encompasses all of the core competencies related to literacy: reading, writing, listening, speaking, editing, revising, presenting, publishing, spelling, punctuating, constructing sentences—every one of the skills that establishes the conditions of a literate person and the foundations for literary communication. Another point here, therefore, is all the missed opportunities for educators to embrace and act on the many pathways to literacy and learning that these students have placed before us. Here are concrete examples—not pliable statistics or overworked theories—of youths who, by the nature of their products and processes, are offering answers to our most elusive educational questions: How do we close the achievement gap? How do we reinforce basic skills? How do we improve high school graduation rates? How do we engage children in learning? How do we make students accountable for what they learn?

To date, most efforts in the field to address these questions have been extracurricular—focusing on issues of class size, funding inequalities, administrative structures, parental involvement, and community resources. These are extremely important matters, all crucial to the improvement of our schools and the young people whom they serve. However, relatively little action has altered what actually transpires in the classroom, those thirty-eight minutes between one shrill bell and the next. Curriculum and all its elements—learning goals, sequences of study, materials and texts, seating arrangements, teaching approaches, assessment tools—have remained largely unchanged. Most classrooms in the United States look and function exactly as they did ten, twenty, fifty, even one hundred years ago: rows of desks, textbooks, a chalkboard, a teacher in the front of the class. If a modern-day Rip Van Winkle were to awaken from a century of sleep, the one and only place where he would likely feel comfortable, the one place most unaffected by technological advancements, social improvements, and ideological changes, would be a school classroom.

If the remedies to our educational illnesses are, as I argue, curricular in nature, then what are the implications of this book—that every student should sit around a table and design comic books? On the contrary, such a unilateral approach to curriculum is simply another incarnation of our current factory-model standard of learning. Rather, this book indicates that (a) young people have a diverse range of interests, many of which challenge trends and stereotypes that we assume to be true, and (b) those interests can become bridges to learning—including the acquisition of difficult content and concepts—if educators embrace them as such. By way of example, a young videogame fanatic can build literacy skills during game play, as James Paul Gee demonstrated.[1] But from a curricular perspective, that young person can also design and produce videogames, thereby writing about the characters, graphing the ratios and proportions of sequential levels, incorporating elements of history and science into the game assets, and using technology to build the game itself. As another example students who love hip-hop music can listen to and analyze their favorite songs. But as I am attempting to demonstrate through a new project called the Youth Music Exchange, they can also form a record label by composing and recording original music and lyrics, writing a marketing plan and press release, developing a balance sheet for profits and expenses, and bringing a youth-generated product to the school and surrounding community. One can imagine similar examples of socially relevant curricula, all with tangible connections to basic academic skills, related to sports, web design, film, animation, dance, environmental sustainability, and as many more as a creative educator can imagine.

Beyond the intractability of schools and school systems, the necessity of a radically transformed role of the teacher may be the most obvious barrier to the adoption of socially relevant curricula. When a learning project is based on publishing manga, for example, and the students are true experts in the field, the students simply know more about the subject than the teacher. A teacher—even Phil DeJean—could not successfully stand before the MLKHS students and lecture them on the history of manga and its role in Japanese society because the students have experienced the content first-hand—they have *lived* the topic. What the teacher can do, however, is establish entry-ways into the project for the academic content and skills that the students are required to learn as mandated by benchmark academic standards. In the manga-based project, then, perhaps a review of compound sentences immediately applied to the dialogue of the characters in the manga. Perhaps a demonstration and discussion on the use of semicolons, one of which must appear in correct usage in the comic book. In this way, a teacher becomes more of an instructional designer than an omniscient imparter of knowledge or an authority figure. The teacher is an expert in one thing, and the students are experts in another. Together they learn; together they teach. The learning experience becomes collaborative and communal rather than unidirectional. And in the end, the job of teaching becomes easier rather than ever more difficult with each passing year.

As discussed specifically in chapter 3 and implied throughout this book, one educational movement has already required such teacher transformations and has adopted socially relevant curricula as the core of its instructional approach: afterschool education. Two aspects of the afterschool environment have established socially relevant learning as a mainstay. First, youth development is a valued goal of afterschool education. Community-based organizations typically aim to help the youths in their communities by offering afterschool programs to keep young people out of trouble, provide them with academic support, and advance the development of social and personal skills required of students in school and, eventually, in the workforce. These programs want children to reflect on who they are and where they live. As a consequence, much of the learning that takes place after school is rooted in the interests and identities of the students who attend the programs. Furthermore, the increasing accessibility of technology is helping afterschool programs establish a variety of offerings that have both academic and social benefits.

The second aspect of socially relevant learning after school is a result of the paradox inherent in afterschool education highlighted in chapter 3. Because enrollment in an afterschool program is not mandatory, children choose the clubs and offerings in which they want to participate. Therefore, in order to maintain enrollment and attendance, afterschool programs are forced to offer the most interesting and socially relevant clubs possible. Fractions club after school would never fly, but fractions within the context of a business plan for an afterschool film company would be perfectly reasonable. There is assuredly no commas club anywhere in the world devoted to the use of the versatile punctuation mark, but working with commas when writing dialogue for a comic book club only makes sense. In essence, children after school are required to learn and improve academically, but they are not required to be there. Hence, the learning opportunities offered after the last bell rings must make children want to attend and, therefore, want to learn. The dichotomy between student learning engagement in school and after school can be astounding, as it was at MLKHS. Unfortunately, one negative result of the success that afterschool programs have achieved in offering socially relevant curricula is that some schools consider themselves less responsible for engaging children in learning. After all, kids get all that "fun" stuff after school.

The relationship between in-school and out-of-school literacies has been researched and documented by many. Notably, Anne Haas Dyson examined young urban children's social worlds, and the literacies contained therein, as a function of their abilities to read and write in school.[2] The two weighty compendia of studies and writing edited by James Flood, Shirley Brice Heath, and Diane Lapp are swollen with examples of school-based reading and writing activities that are supported by the literacies that children choose to embrace out of school.[3] This book stands as another example of literacy in the lives of young people—endeavors in reading, writing, listening, and speaking that endure as personally meaningful and socially relevant for the youths who chose, on their own, to participate. I have also attempted to demonstrate the large extent to which those out-of-school literacies relate to the core competencies and learning standards in English language arts that we tout as the benchmarks of what every student ought to know.

If the comic book club at MLKHS teaches us anything, it is that students are not receptacles for information. They enter our classrooms with diverse experiences, interests, and backgrounds. This is a good thing—each of those experiences, interests, and backgrounds can be mined for a writing project, math exercise, science experiment, or social studies inquiry. Unfortunately, these learning opportunities did not regularly manifest during the school day at MLKHS. The connection between learning and life occurred only after school when the grade books were closed. The club members were well aware of the disparities between the learning environment in school and that after school. In many ways, this chasm served to further distance a number of the club members from their school assignments and the content of their classes. Assuredly the teachers at MLKHS hoped to engage the students to the same extent as the comic book club. But for whatever reasons—administrative pressures, lack of professional development, standardized testing—that seldom happened. As a result, club members withdrew into their comics, these worlds of their own making, and let school pass them by. This is unfortunate and, in fact, unnecessary given the unbridled passion with which these adolescents embraced learning when it meant something to them.

Looking Back to Look Ahead

After walking through the metal detector, the first thing a person sees upon entering MLKHS is a large portrait of Dr. Martin Luther King Jr. His eyes have gazed on the students since the school first opened in 1975, and those eyes have certainly observed much that has changed—hairstyles, clothes, music players. And yet they have witnessed so much more that has remained the same. Despite its location in one of the wealthiest zip codes in the United States, the school building is racially segregated from the neighborhood, nonwhite students accounting for a vast majority of the student body. The students' knapsacks may look different than they did decades ago, but the textbooks inside are remarkably unchanged. Each of the people entering Lincoln Center across the street comes to work with a laptop or sits at a desk with a computer, but not so in Dr. King's building. Saddest of all, the school that once opened in honor of Dr. King was forced to close because of violence, the very thing that the civil rights leader worked tirelessly to combat and that which ended his life so suddenly.

Yet even though our schools have been guilty of ignoring, in Dr. King's words, the "fierce urgency of now" and succumbing to "the tranquilizing drug of gradualism," many good teachers have done and continue to do great things for students with especially difficult lives.[4] These teachers go out of their way to engage such students in learning. They might do some lecturing, but direct instruction is only one of their teaching methods. They give tests, but as a measure of what students have accomplished rather than as a punitive experience. These teachers have discovered what has been called the "art of teaching"—the ability to make students love to learn and want to succeed.

My time with the students at MLKHS highlighted for me just how thirsty these young people were to be engaged in learning experiences. They partially quenched that thirst in the after-school comic book club through the support of Phil DeJean. Yet there were so many extraordinary opportunities to employ their passions for manga— or any other subject meaningful to them—in English, science, social studies, and even math classes during the school day. The only way a teacher could help the students make those connections, however, would be to ask: "So what is your story? What interests you?" These questions and the ensuing answers take time away from planned class lessons. They certainly do not coincide with test preparation. The design of new lessons built around student interests requires more than the standard worksheets and textbooks. But in the end, the opportunities for learning engagement, especially for students who are so parched to be engaged, far outweigh the extra time and effort on the teacher's part.

In considering learning engagement, one cannot forget the impact on teachers. Like a two-way electrical current, teachers who engage students in learning in turn become all the more engaged in teaching because of the excitement put forth by students. Speaking for myself, even though I was not teaching the students at MLKHS, I became inspired through their passion for manga. I began to understand the role of manga in Japanese and American society. I explored the history of manga and its development over time. Like the MLKHS students, I started to pluck manga off the shelves at the bookstore and became enamored with the wit and charm of the literature. I, too, found myself wondering what Naruto would do next, how he would defeat his latest ninja enemy. And through the openness of these students and their willingness to allow me to learn from their lives, I began to understand their passion for Japanese-inspired fantasy. For that, I can only say, *"Domo arigato."*

Appendix A

Anatomy of the Comic Book Club

THERE ARE PRACTICAL IMPLICATIONS of the comic book club at MLKHS, and its success can be a model for other schools and organizations. Of course, there is no right or wrong way to go about it, and different populations of learners require different approaches. Flexibility was certainly one key to the club's achievements. For example, the club did not start with a focus on manga, but the participants' interests impelled the club to move in that direction. As a guideline to the anatomy of the MLKHS model, the following components and conditions were instrumental in launching and sustaining the club.

Designating an Instructor

Phil DeJean was a special person with an extraordinary devotion to comic books and manga, which made him an ideal candidate as instructor for the comic book club. Yet it was not Phil's interest in manga that inspired the students as much as his interest in them as creative people. Especially given the range of writing skills and artistic abilities among the club members, Phil had a knack for motivating every adolescent who exhibited a willingness to learn and a desire to improve regardless of demonstrated abilities at the outset. He provided a structure and process for designing manga, but he frequently told the club members, "Do it your way." The result was a wide array of styles and approaches that individual participants developed for themselves in light of advice, praise, criticism, prodding, and ribbing from surrounding peers. Phil emphasized the relationship between students' input of effort and their output of quality work, and he fostered that equation. A participant who attended regularly and concentrated on weekly improvement received continual attention from Phil. A participant who floated in and out of the club and did not demonstrate much beyond a talent for drawing often received an admonishment from Phil and scowls from peers in the group. Such fickle students usually abandoned the club after a few weeks.

Ideal club instructors, therefore, are educators with the ability to motivate and inspire. They are people who, regardless of their own interests and abilities, can elicit and capitalize on the interest and abilities of the participating youths. I am convinced that such educators need not be artists or art educators. In fact, I have often witnessed comic book clubs led by experienced artists who overwhelm the young participants with their drawing abilities, thereby establishing an unbridgeable gulf between educator and learner. The instructor must be an efficient and accommodating problem-solver, a person who can recognize the needs of the youths before those needs become inhibitors to success. It is not enough to respond when youths ask for help; often they are not sure of how to ask, or even if they require assistance. Phil sensed the needs of students and put forth ideas for them to make their own decisions about how best to problem solve. And, of course, the instructor—as with all educators—needs to be sensitive to the issues in a child's life. Phil was more than generous with his time for club members such as Kischer and Keith. It may seem obvious that caring is a prerequisite for successful teaching, but these two teenagers in particular lacked compassionate adults in their lives, and Phil made a difference.

Recruiting Students

The Opening Doors program first recruited participants for the comic book club by posting flyers and making announcements to the afterschool community at MLKHS, but the program administrators also approached individual students. Rebecca Fabiano in particular had a keen eye for teens who exhibited artistic abilities, especially those who were getting into trouble for drawing when they were supposed to be doing homework or preparing for a test. She recruited students who, like Erick, lacked direction and would benefit from involvement in developing what the comic book club would eventually come to be. The club also welcomed students who were interested in manga and comics but who had never attempted to create their own. Some of the most accomplished club members started in the club with very little experience.

Once students joined the club, the immediately evident amount of commitment and effort necessary for success tended to weed out less-dedicated participants. The leaders of the club, those teenagers who worked extremely hard at designing manga, rarely allowed "slackers," especially those who would boast of their talent but produce hardly anything at all. In contrast, they welcomed and encouraged club participants who devoted as much energy as they, even if novices took some time to develop an idea or style for their comics. Bonds of friendship were quickly formed by the most dedicated club members, but they appreciated newcomers who offered fresh ideas and more manga for the entire group to read. It is important to remember that the club members were drawn from the six discrete schools that shared the same building, all of which remained separate during the school day. The comic book club transcended the violence and animosities that frequently occurred between students from different schools by establishing a hospitable atmosphere for creativity and personal development.

Finding a Space

When the club at MLKHS first launched, it was held in Phil DeJean's art room, a spacious classroom with large tables, chairs, and plenty of light. The tables were arranged in blocks so that students could converge around a table and socialize while they designed their comics, or, alternatively, students could find a relatively quiet spot in the room if they so desired. Often, students would shift between spots in the room—around the table as they brainstormed and drafted, then over to a quiet area when their comic required extreme focus. The tables were strewn with papers and pencils, but conflicts over resources were rare. The students knew where in the room to find more supplies, and they shared willingly. This clubroom also contained a lightbox, which the students used to trace their sketches onto quality paper; a rapidly decaying computer; and a low-end flatbed scanner.

When Phil's position at the school became tenuous in 2007, the comic book club was no longer allowed to meet in the art room after school. It moved instead to the cafeteria, the only other space large enough to accommodate the growing membership of the club. Here were long tables with attached benches, which made collaboration difficult. The fluorescent light was poor. Food wrappers and milk containers dotted the tables. Sticky stains from the day's lunch periods frequently forced the club members to peel their sketchbooks from the tables. Worst of all, however, was the noise. The cavernous cafeteria was a thoroughfare for anyone going to or from the Opening Doors program. Other students sat at the tables to chat or play cards, and at times it was difficult to tell who was in the comic book club and who was simply hanging out. Once the step team began to rehearse on the other side of the cafeteria, hip-hop music blaring from their stereo, it became impossible to have a discussion. Students had to shout at each other to be heard, only adding to the cacophony. Needless to say, the art room was a much more suitable space than the cafeteria for the club. In the art room, the club members were contained and undistracted by outside forces, allowing for open discussion and private thought. The art room was a clubroom; the cafeteria was merely a room, often loud and malodorous. Many students found the move to the cafeteria demeaning, and they resented their ouster from the one space where they could create manga in peace. Outside of MLKHS, I have witnessed a number of different comic book clubs that have convened in a cafeteria, and the placement has worked for none of them.

Scheduling

The club met every Thursday afternoon from about 3:45 to 5:45, with a brief break for snack at 4:30. The question of whether the club should meet more often had arisen, especially given the students' enthusiasm. However, the weeklong break between sessions proved useful for students to reflect on and practice what they had learned during the prior session. They were expected to practice drawing, writing, and inking on the off days, just as dedicated members of the basketball team would practice jump shots and free throws. Club members frequently visited Phil between sessions to ask advice or to get feedback on a drawing or character design. He gave his time willingly, but he also encouraged the students to share their questions with the entire group so that each individual could learn from everyone else's progress. On the days when the club did not meet, the members often assembled at Barnes & Noble to read manga off the shelves and research artistic styles and storylines for their own comics. They brought the information with them on Thursdays and eagerly shared it with their peers. Eventually, as the club grew larger, an anime club began to meet on Tuesday afternoons. It attracted many, though not all, of the same students, who reviewed anime shows and films while other club members continued working on their comics in the back of the room.

Materials and Supplies

Most of what the club members created was accomplished with blank typing paper and lead pencils. Once the loose papers became unwieldy, the students moved to sketchbooks. The sketchbooks also functioned as journals and diaries—a given drawing represented the events and the mood of the day it was created. To ink their pencil art, the students used a variety of black pens, some professional grade and others run of the mill. Students who wanted to add color to their artwork by hand usually did so with colored pencils or occasionally by crayon. When the club met in the art room, Phil provided students with rulers, protractors, and a variety of basic art supplies; when they moved to the cafeteria, these items were less readily available.

The technological assets of the clubroom were paltry, but the students did make use of them. The lightbox enabled students to trace their drawings onto quality paper. Once the "clean" versions were in place and inked, many students opted to scan their artwork at 300 dots per inch (dpi) with the flatbed scanner and then colored their comics on the computer with Adobe Photoshop. Occasionally, the club traveled uptown to Teachers College in order to use the computer lab there, which featured numerous scanners, upgraded computers, and the Adobe Creative Suite on every machine. It was obvious how much more the students would have accomplished had these resources been available at MLKHS.

The most ubiquitous resource in the clubroom was manga. The books teetered in piles on the tables. The students referred to the Tokyopop, Viz, and Dark Horse publications as they created their own stories, or they read the comics as a respite from the arduous task of drafting. The club members certainly had their favorites, listed in appendix C. Based on past experiences with younger comic book creators, I voiced two concerns about focusing on professionally designed comics in the club setting. First, I have seen students with less-developed art skills become frustrated at their inability to create comics as dynamic as those high-end productions. That frustration can completely shutter the creative process. Second, I have seen students with more-developed art skills simply trace the characters that they see before them. Some of the most artistically advanced students never get beyond their robotic regenerations of favorite characters. Neither of these concerns was realized with the club members at MLKHS. The high schoolers already had formulated concepts of how their characters would look and how they would act in the original manga—the professional publications only served to bolster the students' ideas and inspire new storylines.

Publishing and Exhibiting

Aside from the process of creating comics in and of itself, the most exciting aspect of the comic book club for the students was publishing their work in print and online. The publication process drove students to complete their comics, a difficult mission for the perfectionists in the group or for those who struggled to efficiently manage their time. The publications represented a tangible outcome of a year's worth of hard work, and seeing their names in print alongside their comics fostered an inspirational feeling for all of the students who were featured in the publications. A note of caution about printed publications, however: they are expensive, and a printed publication in the first year means that students expect one every year thereafter. The Opening Doors program struggled to fund the publication after the first two years of the comic book club. The Comic Book Project covered half of the printing costs in 2007 from an ever tightening budget, and the entire cost in 2008. Online publishing, on the other hand, is essentially free of cost, and the MLKHS students enjoyed viewing their comics on the Internet and posting them to blogs and other online sources.

The presentations and exhibitions in which the students participated were an opportunity to share their comics with a wider audience. During exhibits for the Comic Book Project at Barnes & Noble, the MLKHS students interacted with children as young as first graders, who were consistently amazed at the high school work. The younger students stood before the poster displays of the manga, pointing fingers at a flying demon here or a samurai warlord there. The MLKHS club members stood next to their posters and explained the details and drawing techniques. They spoke about the storylines and what their characters learned from unworldly experiences. The elementary schoolers grew wide-eyed with each new piece of information, and many of them adopted the MLKHS students as their models for creating comics, yet another generation of urban manga fanatics on the rise. These opportunities reaffirmed for the high schoolers the quality of their work and their ability to enthuse others.

Methodology

THIS BOOK IS BASED ON ETHNOGRAPHIC DATA collected between 2004 and 2008. The goal of the study was to investigate the processes and products of a high school comic book club. The results would inform the field about (a) the successes and challenges experienced by individual participants and the club as a whole, and (b) how the club evolved over time.

Data Collection

Data were collected through the following methods: site observations, video documentation, interviews, and collection of student work.

Site Observations

Over the course of the study, frequent observations of the comic book club were conducted. The purpose of the observations was to collect and organize a wide range of information about the club in order to identify emergent patterns and themes. The observations, which were summarized in written reports immediately following each observation session, were guided by the following questions:

- How did the after-school comic book club begin?
- Who initiated the process?

- What resources—time, personnel, funds, and so on—were made available, and by whom?

- Did site staff receive training specific to the initiative, and from whom?

- How were students recruited to participate in the initiative?

- Who participated? Who did not?

- How did students perceive the initiative, and how did perceptions change over time?

- How did students interact with each other and with the designated teacher?

- What challenges did students and teacher encounter?

- How did students and teachers benefit or improve?

Video Documentation

Digital video documentation was taken at the site. The purpose of the video documentation was to capture key components of the process:

- Introduction of the initiative

- Participants' development of ideas and concepts

- Participants' creation and production of comic books

- Participants' presentation of comic books

Interviews

Interviews with students, teachers, and administrators were conducted throughout the comic book initiative at the site. The purpose was to capture interviewees' expectations and perceptions at each year's launch of the comic book club, their reflections on the club's progress as the year advanced, and perceived successes and failures at the year's conclusion. The interviews were guided by a framework of questions but were open-ended to allow for comprehensive responses from the participants.

Examples of student interview questions at the beginning of the process were:

- Why did you join this club?

- What do you think you will learn from your involvement?

- Have you ever created a comic book before?

- How important are comic books in your life?

- What do you think you will demonstrate about yourself by making a comic book?

- Will your comic book express ideas about your culture or background? If so, how?

Examples of student questions at the end of the process were:

- What did you like most about the process?

- What did you find most challenging?

- What did you learn about yourself through this process?

- What did you learn about your culture or other cultures?

- How do you think your involvement will affect the way you think and act in the future?

Teacher and administrator interviews encompassed not only what the adults believed students had gained or learned, but also what the adults themselves drew from the experience. Administrator interviews also concentrated on the effects of the initiative on the site as a whole, as well as on perceived effects on parents and community members.

Collection of Student Work

Two categories of student work were collected throughout the course of the study: (a) completed comic books that appeared in the annual culminating publications, and (b) sketches and drafts of student comic books in progress.

Data Analysis

The analysis of this data led to identification of emergent themes in the after-school comic book club. The themes were not predetermined; rather they emerged from the data based on the analyses described below:

Observation and Video Analysis

The video documentation and observation reports were analyzed by creating a codebook of themes, actions, and phenomena evident in the data. The codebook was hierarchical though flexible, and it expanded as the data were analyzed. After the initial development of the codebook, NVivo data analysis software was used to code the digital video footage and observation reports. The data were sorted by code and cross-referenced so that conclusions could be drawn about individual students and the club as an entity.

Interview Analysis

To analyze the interview responses, a second codebook was created, parallel to the one from the observation and video analysis. NVivo was again used to code the interview transcripts, and the data were sorted by code and cross-referenced. When analysis of interview data highlighted trends, themes, or phenomena that were unclear or needed more detail, additional interviews were conducted.

Content Analysis

The student-generated comic books were analyzed by creating a third parallel codebook. The same software was used to code the comic books. The data were once again sorted and cross-referenced to provide tangible examples of outcomes of the after-school comic book club.

Appendix C

Club Members' Favorite Manga

Arakawa, Hiromu. *Fullmetal Alchemist*. New York: Viz Media, 2005.

CLAMP. *Clover*. New York: Tokyopop, 2001.

———. *Tsubasa: Reservoir Chronicle*. New York: Del Rey, 2004.

Fujishima, Kosuke. *Oh My Goddess!* Milwaukie, OR: Dark Horse Comics, 2005.

Fukushima, Haruka. *Instant Teen: Just Add Nuts*. New York: Tokyopop, 2004.

Higuri, You. *Cantarella*. Agoura Hills CA: Go! Media Entertainment, 2006.

Hoshino, Katsura. *D.Gray-Man*. New York: Viz Media, 2006.

Kano, Yasuhiro. *Pretty Face*. New York: Viz Media, 2007.

Kishimoto, Masashi. *Naruto*. New York: Viz Media, 2005.

Koike, Kazuo, and Goseki Kojima. *Lone Wolf and Cub*. Milwaukie, OR: Dark Horse Comics, 2000.

Kouga, Yun. *Loveless*. New York: Tokyopop, 2006.

Kubo, Tite. *Bleach*. New York: Viz Media, 2004.

Masamune, Shirow. *Ghost in the Shell*. Milwaukie, OR: Dark Horse, 1995.

Mizushiro, Setona. *After School Nightmare*. Agoura Hills CA: Go! Media Entertainment, 2006.

Murakami, Maki. *Gravitation*. New York: Tokyopop, 2006.

Nakamura, Yoshiki. *Skip Beat!* New York: Viz Media, 2006.

Oh!great. *Air Gear*. New York: Del Rey, 2006.

Shinohara, Chie. *Red River*. New York: Viz Media, 2004.

Sorano, Kaili. *Monochrome Factor*. New York: Tokyopop, 2007.

Takahashi, Rumiko. *Ranma ?*. New York: Viz Media, 2004.

Takamure, Tamotsu. *Jazz*. Gardena, CA: Digital Manga Publishing, 2005.

Takuya, Fujima. *Free Collars Kingdom*. New York: Del Rey, 2007.

Tateno, Makoto. *Yellow*. Gardena, CA: Digital Manga Publishing, 2006.

Ueda, Rinko. *Tail of the Moon*. New York: Viz Media, 2006.

Watsuki, Nobuhiro. *Rurouni Kenshin*. New York: Viz Media, 2006.

Yabuki, Kentaro. *Black Cat*. New York: Viz Media, 2006.

Yazawa, Ai. *Nana*. New York: Viz Media, 2005.

———. *Paradise Kiss*. New York: Tokyopop, 2004.

Yuki, Kaori. *Godchild*. New York: Viz Media, 2006.

Yumeji, Kiriko and Tou Ubukata. *Le Chevalier d'Eon*. New York: Del Rey, 2007.

Notes

Foreword

1. Toon Books, http://www.toon-books.com/about.php.
2. Rodolphe Töpffer, "Essay on Physiognomy" (1845), trans. Ellen Wiese, in *Enter: The Comics— Rodolphe Töpffer's "Essay on Physiognomy" and "The True Story of Monsieur Crepin,"* ed. Ellen Wiese (Lincoln, NE: University of Nebraska Press, 1965), 1–36.

Introduction

1. Art Spiegelman, *The Complete Maus* (New York: Penguin, 2003); and Gene Luen Yang, *American Born Chinese* (New York: First Second Books, 2006).
2. David Booth and Kathleen Lundy, *Boosting Literacy with Graphic Novels* (Orlando, FL: Steck-Vaughn, 2007); Stephen Cary, *Going Graphic: Comics at Work in the Multilingual Classroom* (Portsmouth, NH: Heinemann, 2004); and Michele Gorman, *Getting Graphic: Using Graphic Novels to Promote Literacy with Preteens and Teens* (Columbus, OH: Linworth, 2003).
3. www.teachingcomics.org.
4. W. W. D. Sones, "The Comics and Instructional Method," *Journal of Educational Sociology* 18, no. 4 (1944): 232–240.
5. Steve Duin and Mike Richardson, *Comics: Between the Panels* (Milwaukie, OR: Dark Horse Comics, 2003).
6. Tim Mucci and Rad Sechrist, *Mark Twain's Tom Sawyer* (New York: Sterling, 2008); and Adam Sexton and Tintin Pantoja, *Shakespeare's Hamlet: The Manga Edition* (Hoboken, NJ: Wiley, 2008).
7. Jason Henderson, Tony Salvaggio, and Shane Granger, *Psy-Comm* (New York: Kaplan, 2005), 8.
8. *Superman: Math Made Easy* (New York: Dorling Kindersley Publishing, 2007).
9. Katherine T. Bucher and Lee M. Manning, "Bringing Graphic Novels into a School's Curriculum," *Clearing House* 78, no. 2 (2004): 67; James Bucky Carter, ed., *Building Literacy Connections with Graphic Novels: Page by Page, Panel by Panel* (Urbana, IL: National Council of Teachers of English, 2007); Philip Crawford, "A Novel Approach: Using Graphic Novels to Attract Reluctant Readers and Promote Literacy," *Library Media Connection* 22, no. 5 (2004): 26; Nancy Frey and Douglas Fisher, *Teaching Visual Literacy: Using Comic Books, Graphic Novels, Anime, Cartoons and More to Develop Comprehension and Thinking Skills* (Thousand Oaks, CA: Corwin, 2008); Heidi MacDonald, "Drawing a Crowd: Graphic Novel Events Are Great Ways to Generate Excitement," *School Library Journal* 50, no. 8 (2004): S20; Lorena J. O'English, Gregory Matthews, and Elizabeth Blakesley Lindsay, "Graphic Novels in Academic Libraries: From "Maus" to Manga and Beyond," *Journal of Academic Librarianship* 32, no. 2 (2006): 173–182; and Adam Schwartz and Eliane Rubinstein-Avila, "Understanding the Manga Hype: Uncovering the Multimodality of Comic-book Literacies," *Journal of Adolescent & Adult Literacy* 50, no. 1 (2006): 40–49.

10. Judith M. Burton, Robert Horowitz, and Hal Abeles, "Learning In and Through the Arts: Curriculum Implications," in *Champions for Change: The Impact of the Arts on Learning*, ed. Edward B. Fiske (Washington, DC: Arts Education Partnership, 1999), 35–46.

11. Arts Education Partnership, *Creating Quality Integrated and Interdisciplinary Arts Programs* (Washington, DC: Arts Education Partnership, 2002); and Gail E. Burnaford, Arnold Aprill, and Cynthia Weiss, *Renaissance in the Classroom: Arts Integration and Meaningful Learning* (Mahwah, NJ: Erlbaum, 2001).

12. John Dewey, "My Pedagogic Creed," *School Journal* 54, no. 3 (1897): 77–80.

13. James S. Catterall and Lynn Waldorf. "Chicago Arts Partnerships: Summary Evaluation," in *Champions for Change*, ed. Edward B. Fiske, 47–62; and President's Committee on the Arts and the Humanities and Arts Education Partnership, *Gaining the Arts Advantage: Lessons from School Districts that Value Arts Education* (Washington, DC: Arts Education Partnership, 1999).

14. Paul Gravett, *Manga: Sixty Years of Japanese Comics* (London: Lawrence King, 2003); Adam L. Kern, *Manga from the Floating World: Comicbook Culture and the Kibyoshi of Edo Japan* (Cambridge: Harvard University Press, 2006); Brigitte Koyama-Richard, *One Thousand Years of Manga* (Paris: Flammarion, 2008); Frederick L. Schodt, *Dreamland Japan: Writings on Modern Manga* (Berkeley, CA: Stone Bridge Press, 1996); Frederick L. Schodt, *Manga! Manga! The World of Japanese Comics* (New York: Kodansha, 1986).

15. Brent Wilson, "The Artistic Tower of Babel: Inextricable Links Between Culture and Graphic Development," in *Discerning Art: Concepts and Issues*, eds. George W. Hardman and Theodore Zernich (Champaign, IL: Stipes, 1988); and "Becoming Japanese: Manga, Children's Drawings, and the Construction of National Character," *Visual Arts Research* 25, no. 2 (1999): 48–60.

16. Masami Toku, ed., *Girl Power! Girls' Comics from Japan* (Chico, CA: Flume, 2005); and Masami Toku, "What Is Manga? The Influence of Pop Culture in Adolescent Art," *Art Education* 54, no. 2 (2001): 11–17.

17. CLAMP. *Clover* (New York: Tokyopop, 2001); and Shirow Masamune, *Ghost in the Shell* (Milwaukie, OR: Dark Horse, 1995).

Chapter 1

1. New York State Department of Education, "The New York State School Report Card: Accountability and Overview Report, 2005–06."
https://www.nystart.gov/publicweb-rc/2006/AOR-2006-310300011485.pdf.
https://www.nystart.gov/publicweb-rc/2006/AOR-2006-310300011492.pdf.
https://www.nystart.gov/publicweb-rc/2006/AOR-2006-310300011494.pdf.
https://www.nystart.gov/publicweb-rc/2006/AOR-2006-310300011541.pdf.
https://www.nystart.gov/publicweb-rc/2006/AOR-2006-310300011307.pdf.
https://www.nystart.gov/publicweb-rc/2006/AOR-2006-310300011299.pdf.
https://www.nystart.gov/publicweb-rc/2006/AOR-2006-310500011283.pdf.

2. New York City Department of Education, "Progress Report: 2006-2007."
http://schools.nyc.gov/OA/SchoolReports/2006-07/ProgressReport_HS_M485.pdf.
http://schools.nyc.gov/OA/SchoolReports/2006-07/ProgressReport_HS_M492.pdf.
http://schools.nyc.gov/OA/SchoolReports/2006-07/ProgressReport_HS_M494.pdf.
http://schools.nyc.gov/OA/SchoolReports/2006-07/ProgressReport_HS_M541.pdf.
http://schools.nyc.gov/OA/SchoolReports/2006-07/ProgressReport_HS_M307.pdf.
http://schools.nyc.gov/OA/SchoolReports/2006-07/ProgressReport_HS_M299.pdf.
http://schools.nyc.gov/OA/SchoolReports/2006-07/ProgressReport_HS_M283.pdf.

3. Frederick L. Schodt, *Dreamland Japan: Writings on Modern Manga* (Berkeley, CA: Stone Bridge Press, 1996).

4. Naoko Takeuchi, *Sailor Moon* (New York: Kodansha America, 1995); and Kosuke Fujishima, *Oh My Goddess!* (Milwaukie, OR: Dark Horse Comics, 2005).

5. Brent Wilson, "The Artistic Tower of Babel: Inextricable Links Between Culture and Graphic Development," in *Discerning Art: Concepts and Issues*, eds. George W. Hardman and Theodore Zernich (Champaign, IL: Stipes, 1988), 488–506; Brent Wilson, "Becoming Japanese: Manga, Children's Drawings, and the Construction of National Character," *Visual Arts Research* 25, no. 2 (1999): 48–60.

6. Masami Toku, "What Is Manga? The Influence of Pop Culture in Adolescent Art," *Art Education* 54, no. 2 (2001): 11–17.

7. Japan Ministry of Education. *Course of Study of Lower Secondary School* (Tokyo: Ministry of Education, Science, Sports, and Culture, 1998).

8. Mary Louise Pratt, "Arts of the Contact Zone," in *Ways of Reading*, 4th ed., eds. David Bartholomae and Anthony Petroksky (Boston: St. Martin's Press, 1996), 528–542; and Mary Louise Pratt, *Imperial Eyes: Travel Writing and Transculturation* (New York: Routledge, 1993).

9. Richard J. Deasy, ed., *Critical Links: Learning in the Arts and Student Academic and Social Development* (Washington, DC: Arts Education Partnership, 2002).

10. James S. Catterall and Lynn Waldorf, "Chicago Arts Partnerships: Summary Evaluation," in *Champions for Change: The Impact of the Arts on Learning*, ed. Edward B. Fiske (Washington, DC: Arts Education Partnership, 1999), 47–62; Howard Gardner, "The Happy Meeting of Multiple Intelligences and the Arts," *Harvard Education Letter* 15, no. 6 (1999): 5.

11. Nancie Atwell, *In the Middle: New Understandings About Writing, Reading, and Learning*, 2nd ed. (Portsmouth, NH: Heinemann, 1998); Lucy McCormick Calkins, *The Art of Teaching Writing* (Portsmouth, NH: Heinemann, 1994); Peter Elbow, *Writing with Power: Techniques for Mastering the Writing Process* (New York: Oxford University Press, 1998); and Donald H. Graves, *Writing: Teachers and Children at Work* (Portsmouth, NH: Heinemann: 1983).

Chapter 2

1. Guerrilla Girls, "The Guerrilla Girls' Art Museum Activity Book," http://www.guerrillagirls.com/books/activity.shtml.

2. Alain Locke, *The New Negro* (New York: Albert and Charles Boni, 1925), ix.

3. Bradford W. Wright, *Comic Book Nation: The Transformation of Youth Culture in America* (Baltimore: Johns Hopkins University Press, 2001), 9.

4. See, for example, http://shoujo-manga.com.

5. Museum of Black Superheroes (http://www.blacksuperhero.com/).

6. Adam Kern, *Manga from the Floating World: Comicbook Culture and the Kibyoshi of Edo Japan* (Cambridge: Harvard University Press, 2006); and Frederick L. Schodt, *Dreamland Japan: Writings on Modern Manga* (Berkeley, CA: Stone Bridge Press, 1996).

7. Nami Akimoto, *Miracle Girls* (New York: Tokyopop, 2000).

8. Kosuke Fujishima, *Oh My Goddess!* (Milwaukie, OR: Dark Horse Comics, 2005).

9. Kosuke Fujishima, *Oh My Goddess! Volume 9 TPB*, http://www.darkhorse.com/Books/15-013/Oh-My-Goddess-Volume-9-TPB.

10. Asahina Yuuya, *Love Luck* (Japan: Margaret Comics, 2008).

11. Emily's Random Shoujo Manga Page (http://www.shoujo-manga.com).

Chapter 3

1. Martin L. Gross, *The Conspiracy of Ignorance: The Failure of American Public Schools* (New York: HarperCollins, 1999); E. D. Hirsch Jr., *The Schools We Need and Why We Don't Have Them* (New York: Anchor Books, 1996); Thomas Sowell, *Inside American Education: The Decline, the Deception, the Dogmas* (New York: Free Press, 1993); Maureen Stout, *The Feel-Good Curriculum: The Dumbing Down of America's Kids in the Name of Self-Esteem* (New York: Da Capo Press, 2000); and Charles J. Sykes, *Dumbing Down Our Kids: Why American Children Feel Good about Themselves but Can't Read, Write, or Add* (New York: St. Martin's Press, 1995).
2. Masashi Kishimoto, *Naruto* (New York: Viz Media, 2005).
3. Christopher B. Swanson, *Cities in Crisis: A Special Analytical Report on High School Graduation* (Bethesda, MD: Editorial Projects in Education, 2008).
4. New York State Department of Education, "New York State Learning Standards for English Language Arts," http://www.emsc.nysed.gov/ciai/ela/pub/elalearn.pdf.
5. "Manga Conquers America," *Wired Magazine*, November 2007.
6. Daniel H. Pink, "Japan, Ink: Inside the Manga Industrial Complex," *Wired Magazine*, July 17, 2008, http://www.wired.com/techbiz/media/magazine/15-11/ff_manga.
7. Kenjiro Hata, *Hayate, the Combat Butler* (New York: Viz Media, 2008).
8. Adam Sexton, *Shakespeare: The Manga Edition* (Hoboken, NJ: Wiley, 2008).
9. Gary Martin, *The Art of Comic Book Inking* (Milwaukie, OR: Dark Horse Comics, 1997).

Chapter 4

1. Nancy Beth Jackson, "A Neighborhood Traveled in Dozens of Languages," *New York Times*, July 17, 2005, http://www.nytimes.com/2005/07/17/realestate/17livi.html.
2. New York City Department of Education, "Quality Review Report: 2007–2008." http://schools.nyc.gov/OA/SchoolReports/2007-08/QR_M299.pdf. http://schools.nyc.gov/OA/SchoolReports/2007-08/QR_M492.pdf. http://schools.nyc.gov/OA/SchoolReports/2007-08/QR_M494.pdf. http://schools.nyc.gov/OA/SchoolReports/2007-08/QR_M541.pdf. http://schools.nyc.gov/OA/SchoolReports/2007-08/QR_M283.pdf. http://schools.nyc.gov/OA/SchoolReports/2007-08/QR_M307.pdf.
3. Peter Carey, *Wrong About Japan: A Father's Journey with His Son* (New York: Knopf, 2005).
4. Hayao Miyazaki, director, *Spirited Away* (motion picture) (Japan: Studio Ghibli, 2001).
5. Joyce Gelb, *Gender Policies in Japan and the United States: Comparing Women's Movements, Rights, and Politics* (New York: Palgrave MacMillan, 2003).
6. Masami Toku, ed., *Girl Power! Girls' Comics from Japan* (Chico, CA: Flume, 2005).
7. Machiko Hasegawa, *The Wonderful World of Sazae-san* (New York: Kodansha America, 1997).
8. Steve Leckart, "Wu-Tang Clan's RZA Breaks Down His Kung Fu Samples by Film and Song," *Wired*, November 2007, http://www.wired.com/entertainment/music/magazine/15-11/pl_music; and Jim Jarmusch, director, *Ghost Dog: The Way of the Samurai* (motion picture) (New York: Artisan Entertainment, 1999).
9. Kazuo Koike and Goseki Kojima, *Lone Wolf and Cub* (Milwaukie, OR: Dark Horse Comics, 2000); and Nobuhiro Watsuki, *Rurouni Kenshin* (New York: Viz Media, 2006).
10. New York State Department of Education. "2005–06 Violent and Disruptive Incidents for New York City Public Schools," http://www.emsc.nysed.gov/irts/violence-data/2007/2005-06VADIR-NYC.xls.

11. William C. Thompson, *Audit Report on the Department of Education's Reporting of Violent, Disruptive, and Other Incidents at New York City Public High Schools* (New York: Office of the Comptroller, Bureau of Management Audit, 2007).

12. "What Is the Comic Market? A Presentation by the Comic Market Preparations Committee," http://www.comiket.co.jp/info-a/WhatIsEng080528.pdf.

13. Donna Alvermann and Margaret Hagood, "Fandom and Critical Media Literacy," *Journal of Adolescent and Adult Literacy* 43, no.5 (2000): 436–446.

14. Kelly Chandler-Olcott, "Anime and Manga Fandom: Young People's Multiliteracies Made Visible," in *Handbook of Research on Teaching Literacy Through the Communicative and Visual Arts*, vol. 2, eds. James Flood, Shirley Brice Heath, and Diane Lapp (New York: Erlbaum, 2008), 247–257.

15. jigokushoujo01, *Romeo and Juliet: Tales Before the Tragedy*, http://www.fanfiction.net/s/4340791/1/Romeo_and_Juliet_Tales_Before_the_Tragedy.

16. Rebecca W. Black, "Access and Affiliation: The Literacy and Composition Practices of English-language Learners in an Online Fanfiction Community," *Journal of Adolescent & Adult Literacy* 49, no. 2 (2005): 118–128.

17. Barbara J. Guzzetti and Margaret Gamboa, "Zines for Social Justice: Adolescent Girls Writing on Their Own," *Reading Research Quarterly* 39, no. 4 (2004): 408–436.

18. Takashi Murakami, *Little Boy: The Arts of Japan's Exploding Subculture* (New York: Japan Society, 2005).

19. Brent Wilson, "Child Art, Multiple Interpretations, and Conflicts of Interest" in *Child Development in Art*, ed. Anna M. Kindler (Reston, VA: National Art Education Association, 1997), 86.

Chapter 5

1. Abby Goodnough, with Robert F. Worth, "Latest Shootings Add to King High School's Reputation for Turbulence," January 17, 2002, http://query.nytimes.com/gst/fullpage.html?res=9400E5DC1138F934A25752C0A96496.

2. www.comicbookproject.org/clev05a.htm.

3. Patricia Ayala, *Marcos Movement: El Movimiento de Marcos* (Philadelphia: Xlibris, 2003).

4. Harold E. Hinds and Charles M. Tatum, *Not Just for Children: The Mexican Comic Book in the Late 1960s and 1970s* (Westport, CT: Greenwood Press, 1992).

Chapter 7

1. Yutaka Izubuchi, director, *Rahxephon: Complete Collection* (DVD series) (Houston, TX: ADV Films, 2005).

2. The Youngest Witnesses (http://www.youngestwitnesses.com).

Chapter 9

1. Katsura Hoshino, *D.Gray-Man* (New York: Viz Media, 2006).

2. Murasaki Shikibu, *The Tale of the Genji*, trans. Royall Tyler (New York: Penguin Classics, 2003).

Chapter 12

1. Kubo Tite, *Bleach* (New York: Viz Media, 2004); Hoshino, Katsura, *D.Gray-Man* (New York: Viz Media, 2006); and Yuki Kaori, *Godchild* (New York: Viz Media, 2006).

Chapter 15

1. James Paul Gee, *What Video Games Have to Teach Us About Literacy and Learning*, 2nd ed. (New York: Palgrave MacMillan, 2007).

2. Anne Haas Dyson, *The Brothers and Sisters Learn to Write: Popular Literacies in Childhood and School Cultures* (New York: Teachers College Press, 2002); *Social Worlds of Children Learning to Write in an Urban Primary School* (New York: Teachers College Press, 1993); and *Writing Superheroes: Contemporary Childhood, Popular Culture, and Classroom Literacy* (New York: Teachers College Press, 1997).

3. James Flood, Shirley Brice Heath, and Diane Lapp, eds. *Handbook of Research on Teaching Literacy Through the Communicative and Visual Arts*, vol. 1 (New York: Macmillan, 1997); and *Handbook of Research on Teaching Literacy Through the Communicative and Visual Arts*, vol. 2 (New York: Erlbaum, 2008).

4. Martin Luther King Jr., "I Have a Dream," http://www.stanford.edu/group/King/publications /speeches/address_at_march_on_washington.pdf.

Acknowledgments

THIS BOOK WOULD NOT HAVE BEEN POSSIBLE without the inspirational efforts and achievements of the comic book club members at Martin Luther King Jr. High School in New York City and the adults who have supported them, especially Phil DeJean, Rebecca Fabiano, and Patricia Ayala. Thanks also to Shonda Streete, Susan Bobb, Unique Fraser, Judith Souvenir, Andrea Kamins, and Alena Williams.

Hal Abeles and Judy Burton—codirectors of the Center for Arts Education Research at Teachers College, Columbia University—have granted me invaluable support, mentorship, and guidance over the years. Also at Teachers College—past and present—Arthur Levine, Darlyne Bailey, Jack Hyland, Graeme Sullivan, Lenore Pogonowski, Randall Allsup, Rob Horowitz, Renee Cherow O'Leary, Alice Wilder, Betsy Currier, Paul Kran, Ashley Bogosian, Ravi Ahmad, Erin Weeks-Earp, Rocky Schwarz, Steve Grady, and Danny Vazquez.

Thank you to David Harris, Corrie Heneghan, Nicole Wiltrout, and Ethan Gray at The Mind Trust for supporting me and welcoming me into their family. Also in Indianapolis, the friendliest place on earth, Bart Peterson, Eugene White, Don Stinson, Debbie Sullivan, Steve Papesh, Scott Bess, Randall Glenn, Simon Crookall, Beth Perdue-Outland, Matt Carter, Shaila Mulholland, and Steve and Barb Tegarden.

My gratitude to Peter Mercer, Beth Barnett, Samuel Rosenberg, Alex Urbiel, and the Teacher Education faculty at Ramapo College.

The After-School Corporation (TASC) in New York City has been an enormous champion. Thank you to Lucy Friedman, Charissa Fernandez, Chris Whipple, Sandra DuPree, Stefan Zucker, Kim Baranowski, and all of the site directors and club instructors who have supported the Comic Book Project from the very beginning.

Thank you to Dark Horse Comics for their collaboration—Mike Richardson, Anita Nelson, Nick McWhorter, Monique Sevy, Sarah Robertson, Mark Bernardi, Chris Gaslin, Kim Schettig, and Kendra Sundberg.

Jim Davis and the team at the Professor Garfield Foundation—Bob Levy, Larry Smith, and Madelyn Ferris—have been extraordinary.

The list of individuals who have supported me could fill an entire book, so thank you to everyone who has been a part of the Comic Book Project, Youth Music Exchange, and anything else in which I've had a hand. Special gratitude to Bill McKinney, Andre Worrell, Susan Robeson, Barbara Salander, Carmen Colon, Doug Tarnopol, Sara Hill, Linda Hirsch, Masami Toku, Victoria Lopez, Pamela Konkol, Lori Campos, Marnie Annese, Gloria Savino, Moxie Stoermer, Fabian Leo, Nancy Young Wright, Marge Pellegrino, Kevin Lopez, Cari Wright, Scott Cabot, Pernell Brice, Françoise Mouly, Brian Lehrer, Allen Smith, Brent Staples, Elissa Gootman, Adam Sternbergh, Beth Fertig, Ed Finkel, Pola Rosen, Kathy Satterfield, Pat Kelly, Vicki Carr, David Brown, Deborah Johnson, Donna Guthrie, Nicole Blackham, Ila Jain, Randall Quan, Susan Karwoska, Patrick McLaughlin, Lynn Pinder, Jordi Torrent, Rod Gilchrist, Maryann Fleming, Hank Linhart, Sharon Dunn, Antoin Toniolo, Brent Wilson, Scott Cumbo, Greg Robinson, Will Wilkie, Brian Martin, John Jansen, Gina Gagliano, John Shableski, James Bucky Carter, Eric Zuckerman, Robin Feinman, Julia Hirschberg, Bob Coyne, Eric Gurna, Tom Kurzanski, Dan Jeselsohn, and Danny Anker.

Also, thank you to Danielle Moss Lee, Merle McGee, and the Harlem Educational Activities Fund; Jane Quinn, Sarah Jonas, Janice Chu-Zhu, and the Children's Aid Society; Jennifer Stark and Barnes & Noble; Adam Rabiner, Mike Dogan, and the NYC Department of Youth and Community Development; Yvonne Brathwaite, Ellen O'Connell, Shelly Wilson, Emi Gittleman, and the Partnership for After School Education; Margaret Hagood, Emily Skinner, and the College of Charleston; Tammy Papa, Judy Marella, and the Bridgeport Lighthouse Program; James Sturm, Michelle Ollie, and the Center for Cartoon Studies; Karen Clark-Keys, Sandra Noble, Sherri Pittard, and the Cleveland Metropolitan School District; Peter Guttmacher and the DC Children and Youth Investment Trust Corporation; Lambert Shell, Leslie Taylor and the Queens Public Library; Aaron Dworkin and After-School All-Stars; *Teaching Tolerance* and the Southern Poverty Law Center; Vanessa Francisco and the Central Park Conservancy; Barbara Ferman, Catie Cavanaugh, and the University Community Collaborative of Philadelphia at Temple University; Pat Donohue and the Bonner Center for Civic and Community Engagement at the College of New Jersey; Kevin McGowan and the Bonner Scholars Corp at Middlesex County College; Brenda Manuelito, Dedra Buchwald, Jonathan Tomhave, and Native People for Cancer Control at the University of Washington; Angela Nelson, Charles Coletta, and the Department of Popular Culture at Bowling Green State University; Rebkha Atnafou, Lori Carter, Nicole Carter, and the After-School Institute in Baltimore; Carmen Vega-Rivera, Martine King, and Say Yes to Education; Philadelphia Safe and Sound; After School Matters in Chicago; AdGraphics; and the book's copyeditor Monica Jainschigg.

My work has been supported by a number of generous foundations: the Cleveland Foundation, Union Square Awards, Robert Bowne Foundation, Corporation for National and Community Service, JPMorgan Chase Foundation, HSBC Foundation, and the US Airways Education Foundation.

A special thank you to the Bitz, Rubin, Gold, and Dienstfrey families.

About the Author

DR. MICHAEL BITZ, EDD, is the founder of the Comic Book Project (www.Comic BookProject.org) and cofounder of the Youth Music Exchange (www.Youth Music Exchange.org). He is the first recipient of the Educational Entrepreneurship Fellowship at the Mind Trust in Indianapolis, and he received the Distinguished Alumni Early Career Award from Teachers College, Columbia University. His innovative pathways to learning have impacted children worldwide and have been featured by the *New York Times*, *Washington Post*, National Public Radio, and many others. Dr. Bitz has served on the faculty at Teachers College, Columbia University and Ramapo College.

Index

Information contained in figures and tables are indicated by an italic *f* and *t* respectively.